COVERED CALL FOR BEGINNERS

GAIN MONTHLY INCOME WITH SHARES

MAXIMIZE YOUR PROFITS WITH OPTIONS

COVERED CALL FOR BEGINNERS

GAIN MONTHLY INCOME WITH SHARES

MAXIMIZE YOUR PROFITS WITH OPTIONS

1st Edition

Rubens Gonçalves de Souza

NATIONAL LIBRARY OF AUSTRALIA

A catalogue record for this book is available from the National Library of Australia

Legal Notice

The content contained or made available in this book is not intended and does not constitute investment advice. The author is providing this book and its content for informational and educational purposes only. The material presented herein is not intended to be a suggestion about trading or an investment recommendation. The use of the information in this book is at your own risk.

The examples in this book are theoretical and are not or may not be accurate, and many examples are suppositions used only to illustrate the explanations. Thus, the author does not give any warranty for the reliability of the information provided within this book.

Trading securities on the stock exchange may involve high risk and the loss of all invested value. The investment information provided in this material may not be appropriate for all investors and is provided without regard to the financial sophistication of each investor, financial situation, investment time horizon or risk tolerance.

Thank you for purchasing this book! Please be so kind as to leave a review when you're done.

Also, feel free to check out our website The Strategist Invest at:
THESTRATEGISTINVEST.COM

Contents

❖ Introduction

For most people who invest in the stock market, there are generally only two ways to generate profit: one, with the dividend paid by the company to the holder of the asset and two, with the appreciation of that asset—that is, the stock must rise.

In this book, you will learn a third alternative to increase the yield of your shares, which is with the use of options. It consists of a more sophisticated style of investing, in which it is possible to make the most of the income potential that your shares can generate. I'll show you how to get high gains even if the stock depreciates or stagnates and how to reduce the risk in your portfolio in the event of a market downturn.

When it comes to risk management, most books on derivatives recommend buying options as insurance, which can erode the gains you have earned with your asset. It is challenging to know when there will be a fall in the market and when it is necessary to buy that insurance (market timing).

This book will address a different concept; instead of buying, you'll sell options and learn how to use your assets to get a steady income. In addition to providing returns, this strategy helps to reduce the initial cost of these assets, which consequently generates a risk reduction.

The goal of every entrepreneur is to increase their income or cash flow, and with the investor, the same aim applies. I'll show you how to use your shares to generate extra income in your portfolio, a payment that could be weekly, monthly, quarterly, or semiannual; all will depend on the way you implement this strategy.

With the help of a great ally, compound interest, this strategy can make a significant difference in your long-term financial investments.

Albert Einstein described compound interest as the most powerful force in the universe and stated that he considered them the eighth Wonder of the World. Said Einstein, "He who understands it earns it; he who doesn't, pays it."

I will explain this strategy simply so that readers who have never heard of options can learn about it. I will also provide more advanced examples and information to help laypeople become experts. Finally, for those who already know the strategy, this book will help you expand your knowledge and see different ways of implementation and management methods.

Now there is no need to wait for the market to rise for you to profit. I'm talking about the sale of the covered call, a low-risk strategy in the equity market. Several other names are given to this strategy, such as " Covered Call" or "Covered Call Writing".

Congratulations! With a bit of dedication, you will learn how to use an excellent tool to invest and maximize the returns in your portfolio.

For any questions regarding this book, please visit: THESTRATEGISTINVEST.COM

1

A Brief History of How Options Came About

History shows two moments when the use of options occurred for perhaps the first time: the first, a strategy used by Thales of Miletus, and the second, the tulip bubble of 1637.

Aristotle mentions Thales in his work "Politics", written around 350 BCE. Aristotle refers to Thales in a section describing how to achieve a monopoly in any aspect of a business.

The story is that Thales, an avid philosopher and astrologer, used his knowledge in mathematics and astrology to predict that the following year's olive harvest would be more abundant than usual. Once the olives were harvested, they needed to be processed with presses, and he predicted that the demand for the presses could increase substantially.

Thales negotiated with the owners of the presses and asked them to sell him the right to use them during the next harvest season, offering in return a small deposit (premium) to secure this right at an agreed price.

The owners accepted it because if Thales decided to use the presses, he would also pay the regular price that all producers paid. However, if he chose not to use them, the owners would keep the deposit paid and could rent the presses to other producers, as they did every year.

In the end, Thales was right, and the following year was a great harvest that saw a massive production of olives. As he owned the right to use the presses, Thales managed to sell the rights on to other producers and made a considerable profit.

Although the term "option contract" was not used at the time, Thales of Miletus may have created the first call option contract, with olive presses as the underlying asset.

One of the most notable uses of options contracts in history occurred in 1637 in the Netherlands during the tulip bubble—that's right, a flower. The tulip became popular and gained prominence as a status symbol because the flower was popular with the Dutch aristocracy, a trend that eventually spread throughout Europe.

Demand for tulips grew so much that many producers and investors entered into options and futures contracts. A secondary market was even created, such as the stock exchange, in which people could speculate on price. The producers borrowed a lot of money; many of them used their own homes as collateral to invest in their tulip plantations.

With so much speculation and leverage occuring, the result couldn't be any different; demand suddenly ran out and the bubble burst. Many people lost their homes, which resulted in one of the most significant recessions in Dutch history. At that time, options contracts were not regulated as they are today, and many were not fulfilled.

The New York Stock Exchange was created in 1971; during this time, to find buyers and sellers of options, the brokers' representatives met at the business desk and sometimes even disclosed the options contracts in newspaper advertisements to attract investors.

The options market continued to expand, but it was not yet standardized, contracts did not have the same expiration dates, and the terms were different, which made trading very difficult.

From 1973, a new world emerged for investors. CBOE, the Chicago Board Options Exchange, was the first exchange to standardize contracts to improve liquidity.

Today, all company contracts have the same expiry date; each contract has come to correspond to the amount of 100 shares; and the standardization rules have also been defined by the stock exchange, where options are marketed.

The internet and the growing number of online brokers and standardization helped expand the use of options, which continues to grow in popularity in the United States and worldwide.

Blank Page

2

Covered Call Writing - Concept

Let's learn how the call option works. First, suppose you buy an asset, such as land or shares. Next, you sell to someone else the right—but not the obligation—to purchase that asset from you, at a certain price that you determine and on a specific date, which you also choose. In return, you receive a cash premium, which is immediately available in your account.

2.1 Real Estate Market - Land

Let's use the real estate market in this example just to illustrate the concept. Suppose investor Ana bought a plot of land in Queensland, Australia, for $100,000. After doing the research, she is confident that this property price will increase because new tourism developments can be built in the area. For this reason, she is determined to sell this land in the future for $130,000.

Joseph, another investor, is excited and very interested in her property. He believes that the land's value can reach up to $160,000 if the local government approves the construction of tourism developments in the area, such as hotels and resorts, which would be decided in the next six months.

Joseph wants to buy the land, but at the same time, he does not want to take a risk and pay the amount of $130,000, the price she is asking.

To find a solution, he offers a deposit of $10,000 for the right to buy the land at $130,000 and the right to decide whether to make the purchase or not in up to six months.

Ana accepts the proposal, and Joseph deposits the $10,000 into her account. Regardless of whether or not Joseph decides to buy the land in the next six months, this deposit belongs to Ana.

Now also imagine that, around the same area, there are neighbors with land identical to Ana, of the same size and costing $100,000. However, they (the neighbors) are not interested in this type of options contract, so Joseph makes a deal with Ana. Below are the terms of the agreement between Joseph and Ana.

Land Option Contract
Premium or Deposit: $10,000
Contract Duration: 6 months
Sales Price / Right to Buy: $130,000

Joseph has up to six months to decide whether to buy the land or not. The deadline can be from one day after closing the contract until the last day, at the end of six months.

No matter what Joseph's decision is, in any of the scenarios, the $10,000 premium belongs to Ana. Now let's look at three possible outcomes after six months when the contract expires.

- ❖ **Scenario 1 (after six months)** - Project **Not Approved:**
  The land consequently depreciates.

- ❖ **Scenario 2 (after six months)** - **Undefined Project:**
  The land price remains stable because the approval of the tourism project was not decided within six months.

- ❖ **Scenario 3 (after six months)** - **Project Approved:**
  The land is valued.

Let's analyze Ana, Joseph, and the neighbors' situation in each of these scenarios.

Scenario 1 - Project Not Approved

With the non-authorization for the leisure construction projects, all the land plots in that area suffer a devaluation. In this scenario, the land is now worth $90,000 on the market. Let's analyze each of the participant's situation.

Land Market Value: $90,000.
Right to buy: Joseph does not exercise the right to purchase.
Joseph: Loses the $10,000.
Ana: Retains her land now at $90,000 and the premium of $10,000.
Neighbors: Retains their land now at $90,000.

In this case, Joseph does not exercise the option to buy for $130,000, according to the contract, because he can buy another plot of similar land on the market for a lower price, the current value of $90,000. So, he loses all the money he invested, which is the premium of $10,000 paid to Ana.

Ana gets the premium of $10,000 and retains her property, now at the market value of $90,000. The neighbors, in this scenario, had their equity reduced from $100,000 to $90,000.

Although the land has devalued, Ana is in a much better situation than the other investors (neighbors), who did not use the options tool. She keeps the equity at $100,000, as it continues with the land that is now worth $90,000 and gets the premium paid by Joseph, of $10,000.

Scenario 2 - Undefined Project

After six months, the project remains undefined in this scenario, and the land price remains stable, at $100,000 on the market.

Land Market Value: $100,000
Right to buy: Joseph does not exercise the right to purchase
Joseph: Loses the $10,000
Ana: Retains the land at $100,000 and the premium of $10,000
Neighbors: Retain the land at $100,000

After six months, the uncertainty about the project continues; Joseph obviously does not exercise the option to buy for $130,000 (according to the contract) because there is similar land on the market, such as the neighbors', for $100,000. Again, he loses all the money he invested, which is the $10,000 premium paid to Ana.

Ana again keeps the $10,000 premium paid by Joseph and retains her property, which remains at the market value of $100,000. As a result, her total equity increased to $110,000, which resulted in an additional income of 10% in six months or 20%, if we consider the annualized value.

The neighbors, in this scenario, kept the equity in the same amount of $100,000 without any additional income.

Scenario 3 - Project Approved

In this scenario, the project is approved, the land had a substantial price increase, as Joseph predicted, and is now worth $160,000 on the market.

Land Market Value: $160,000
Right to buy: Joseph exercises the right to buy

Joseph:
Buys it for $130,000
Sells it for $160, 000
Gain $30, 000
(-) $10,000 of the premium
Profit: $20,000

Ana:
Sells for $130,000
She bought it for $100, 000
Holds: $10,000 of the premium
Profit: $40,000

Neighbors:
Sold for $160, 000
Bought it for $100, 000
Profit: $60,000

Joseph now exercises the right to buy. In this case, the option is exercised, even though the land market price is now $160,000. Ana is assigned (receives an assignment note) and must sell it to Joseph for $130,000 because that's her obligation, according to the contract terms.

Thus, Joseph will buy the land from Ana for the agreed price of $130,000, and he can sell the same land on the market for $160,000. If he decides to do so, Joseph's profit on this transaction will be $30,000, but he also paid $10,000 for the option contract; therefore, Joseph's final yield is $20,000.

Ana bought the land for $100,000 and had to sell it to Joseph for $130,000, earning $30,000 and keeping the premium of 10,000, obtaining a total profit of $40,000. Thus, this transaction generated a return of 40% in six months or 80% annually.

The neighbors, however, bought the land for $100,000 and sold for $160,000, a profit of $60,000 and a return of 60% in six months or 120% annualized.

This is the only scenario in which the performance of the neighbors, who did not opt for the options contract, exceeds Ana's.

Even so, Ana still got an excellent return in scenario three. It is important to remember that the market does not always rise. It has three directions: up, down, and stagnant.

Ana obtained a good result in all scenarios, even in scenario one, in which there was a fall in the property price. Still, her total equity was not affected because the loss was offset by the premium received from the sale of the option contract.

It is worth remembering that because Ana holds the asset (land), there is no added risk in using the option contract. The risk is always in the acquired asset (the land devaluing) and not in the option.

2.2 Stock Market

Let's now apply the concept to the share market. In this example, Ana buys 100 shares of Company XYZ at $50 per share, a total of $5,000. She intends to sell these shares for at least $52 each.

After a week and with good news regarding Company XYZ, Joseph is interested because he believes these shares can appreciate significantly in the next month.

However, he is just speculating and does not want to invest a total of $5,000 to buy the 100 shares, or maybe he does not have all this value available. So he again seeks Ana for a deal. Everything is done using an online broker in real life, and people do not need to know each other.

So, Joseph and Ana enter into a contract. Ana sells an option contract to Joseph, an option known as " call", which gives the buyer of the option the right but not the obligation to buy the shares at the agreed or chosen price. They agree on the shares sales price of $52 and the value of $2 per option, with each option equivalent to one share.

As there are 100 shares, the option contract's value is $200, as it refers to 100 options underlying the 100 shares. The exercise price or strike price is $52; this is the price that Ana wants to sell the shares anyway, with an expiration of one month.

In this contract, Joseph has one month to decide whether or not to exercise the option (his right) to buy the 100 shares at the asking price of $52 per share. The following are the terms of the contract;

XYZ Stock: 1 Option Contract - *Equivalent to 100 shares*
Premium or Deposit: *$200 (unit value $2 x100)*
Contract Duration: *1 month*
Selling price / Exercise Right: *$52 per share (100 shares $5,200)*

In addition to Ana, other investors also bought 100 shares of XYZ company for $50 each share, a total investment of $5,000, but they are not interested in options contracts.

Let's imagine three possible outcomes after a month. Joseph has until the end of the 30 days to decide whether to buy the shares or not.

No matter what Joseph's decision is, in any of the scenarios, Ana will receive and keep the premium of $200.

❖ **Scenario 1 (after 30 days) – Shares depreciate**

❖ **Scenario 2 (after 30 days) – Shares stagnate**

❖ **Scenario 3 (after 30 days) – Shares appreciate**

Scenario 1 – Shares depreciate in price

In this scenario, the company performs poorly, and the shares depreciate from $50 to $48. As a result, the total amount of equity invested in the 100 shares falls to $4,800.

Shares - Market Value: $4,800
Right to buy: Joseph does not exercise the right to buy at $52 per share
Joseph: Loses the total amount invested, premium of $200
Ana: Retains her shares, now at $4,800 and the premium of $200
Other investors: Retains their shares, now at $4,800

In this scenario, Joseph does not exercise the right to buy the shares for $52 because he can go to the market and pay the current lower price, $48 per share. He then loses the premium of $200, and the option expires without value.

Ana saw her investment depreciate to $4,800, but as she gets the premium of $200, she can thus keep her equity in the total amount of $5,000. In addition, she achieved a yield of 4% in one month or 48% annualized.

The return calculation is the premium of $200 divided by the initial investment of $5,000 and then multiplied by 100 to find the percentage.

Now that 30 days have passed, Ana can sell another option in the following month and generate a regular income.

She is in a much better situation than the other investors, who did not use options and saw their equity depreciate from $5,000 to $4,800 in this example.

Scenario 2 - Shares stagnate

In this scenario, nothing interesting happened in the market; XYZ's stock price did not move much and closed at $51, an appreciation of $1 per share at the end of the 30 days.

Shares - Market Value: $5,100
Right to buy: Joseph does not exercise the right to buy at $52 per share
Joseph: Loses the total amount invested, the premium of $200
Ana: Retains her shares, now at $5,100 and the premium of $200
Other investors: Retains their shares, now at $5,100

In this scenario, Joseph again does not exercise the right to buy the shares for $52 because he can go to the market and pay less, the current price of $51 per share.

The slight appreciation of the stock from $50 to $51 was not enough. So again, he loses the premium of $200, and the option expires without value.

However, Ana keeps both the shares worth $51 each, a total value of $5,100, and the premium received of $200, obtaining again a return of 4% in a month or 48% per year.

Her total equity is now worth $5,300, and she can sell another option on the market. What if she did this every month? Remember, the equity of other investors increased to $5,100 without any additional income.

Scenario 3 – Shares appreciate

Joseph was correct in his forecast, and XYZ's share values reach $56 per share in this scenario.

Shares - Market Value: *$5,600*
Right to buy: *Joseph exercises his right to buy at $52 per share. Ana is assigned and has to sell the shares to Joseph for $52.*

Joseph:
Buy the shares for $5,200
Sell the shares on the market for the current price of $5,600
Gain $400
(-) $200 premium
Profit: $200

Ana*:*
Initially bought the shares for $5,000
Now sell them for $5,200
Gain $200
(+) $200 premium
Profit: $400

Other investors*:*
Initially bought the shares for $5,000
They now sell them at the market price of $5,600
Profit: $600

Thus, Joseph will exercise the option, his right to buy, and Ana will receive an assignment note. It means she has been assigned and must sell her shares for the unit value of $52 to Joseph, even though the stock's current market value is $56, because this is her obligation, according to the contract terms.

Joseph will then buy each share for $52, and he can sell the shares on the market at $56, making a profit of $4 per share, for a gain of $400 in this transaction. However, it is still necessary to subtract the amount of $200 that Joseph paid for the options contract, thus leaving him a profit of $200.

Ana initially bought the 100 shares for the unit value of $50 and now sold them to Joseph for $52, which generates a profit of $2 per share, a total of $200 and, with the additional $200 of the option premium paid by Joseph, she obtained a total profit of $400.

The other investors bought the 100 shares at $50 each and sold for $56 without using the options market. In this scenario, the other investors had a total profit of $600, higher than Ana's total profit of $400.

As they say, in the financial market, there is no such thing as a free lunch. To win something, you have to give up something else. Ana did not enjoy the high appreciation of the shares in this scenario to obtain a constant and regular income.

This book will cover the best scenarios for implementing this strategy.

Note that despite having a lower return this time, Ana maintained a positive balance in all three scenarios. That's the great message I intend to send with this book. As I said earlier, the market has three directions: up, down, or stagnant. The covered call vendor benefits from all scenarios.

It is worth remembering again that, in this strategy, the risk is always in the asset (the share or land, as in the previous example) if it depreciates too much. There is no added risk with the sale of the option if the investors already own the shares.

Important note: Selling the call without having the stock in the portfolio is a high-risk strategy. This is called naked call selling and is not recommended in this book.

The following charts are a visual representation comparing when the investor buys only the shares versus buying the shares and selling the call.

Figure 1 is a visual representation of risk and potential gain with the asset without selling the call. Figure 2 shows the stock with the sale of the covered call.

Note that in Figure 1, in which the investor only owns the stock, the profit line has no upward limit in case of appreciation of the stock.

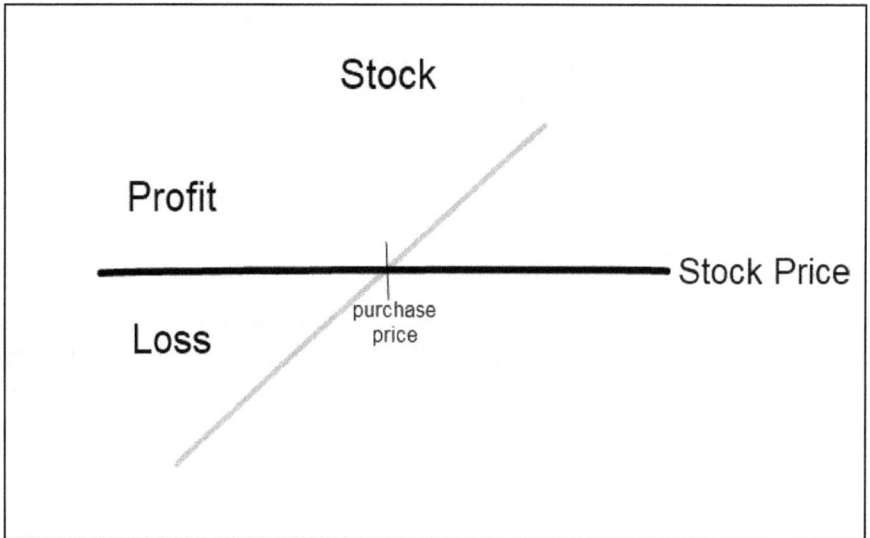

Figure 1: Graph Stock Only

In Figure 2, the investor has a gain limit in case of high appreciation of the asset. However, this limit is offset by an extra yield.

In Figure 1, any devaluation of the stock is a loss, but now in Figure 2, the stock can decrease in value a little, and the investor can still profit. This is because of the additional income from the option premium, which decreases risk.

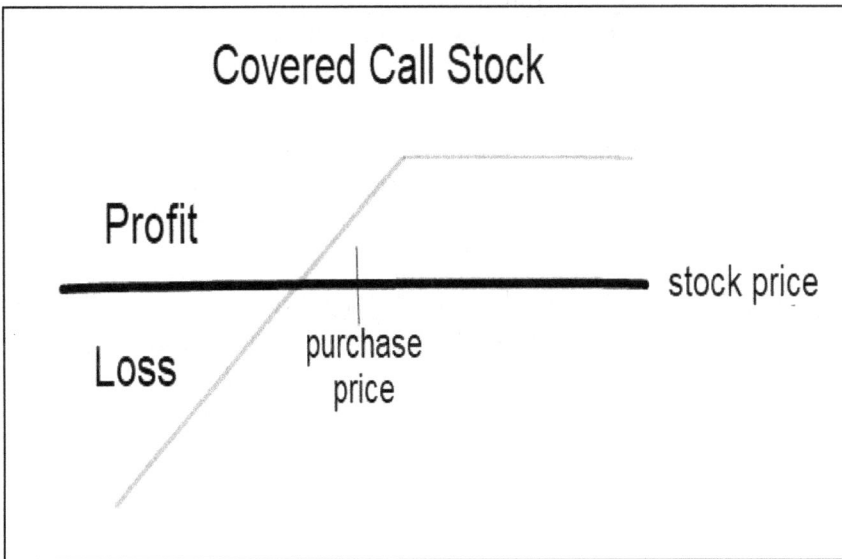

Figure 2: Stock with the Sale of a Call Option - Covered Call

2.3 Chapter Summary

❖ The added sale of the call is risk zero if you already own the stock. However, a strategy that is composed of the share and the sale of the call option is not a risk-free strategy because the risk is always in the asset (shares), with or without the option.

❖ The covered call sales strategy provides extra income and decreases risk, but in return, it limits the earning potential in the event of a significant rise in the asset price.

❖ No extra money is required to sell the call if you already own the stock. In fact, you're getting paid to sell the call.

❖ If you believe that the shares you own can appreciate significantly, selling the covered call option is not advisable.

❖ It is an excellent strategy to generate income and, at the same time, reduce risk.

3

Elementary Definitions

Now that you understand how call options work, in the following section, implementing the strategy, let's look at more examples of how to determine the exercise price, manage the position, and understand when the strategy is more aggressive or defensive.

But before that, some definitions and options features need to be explained. I will describe them simply and, at the same time, provide a guide with more advanced details so that you have all the information on how to manage this strategy more effectively.

Many people buy options, but as mentioned in the introduction, in this book you will learn how to be an option seller who generates income and decreases the risk of their stock by selling the covered call option.

Now we need to know how the option price is calculated.

3.1 Definition: Stock Options

A share option is a contract in which the option buyer has the right—but not the obligation—to buy or sell a particular asset underlying the option, such as a stock, ETF or index.

In the case of the call, it is the right buy, and in the case of the put option, it is the right to sell, at the fixed price established in the contract (strike price), for a certain period, when the contract expires (expiration).

The buyer is also called the **holder**, who can decide to exercise the right to buy or not; the buyer pays the premium for the option.

The seller, who receives the premium, has no rights but rather the obligation to commit to the contract terms and is also called the **option's writer**.

In this book, we will work with the call option, in which we will be the writer or seller, who is the one who receives a premium from selling the right to someone to buy our shares, at a specific strike or exercise price, within a certain time.

At the end of the book, I'll explain some more about the put option, but this is not part of our strategy.

The **premium** is the amount paid by the buyer to the seller. The term **strike or exercise price** is the agreed price between both parties, at which the buyer may or may not exercise the right of purchase.

3.2 Assignment vs Exercise

The call option buyer can **exercise** their right to buy the underlying asset at or before the expiration by contacting the brokerage company.

When the buyer exercises their right to buy the shares, the brokerage company then decides which option seller will get the assignment notification; the assigned person will then have the shares called away and must sell the stock for the strike price of the option contract.

If the seller sold a naked call option (uncovered), this investor would have a short stock position.

3.3 Derivative

The underlying asset is usually a share or stock but can be an ETF or an index. The option contract does not exist without these assets.

The option price derives and is influenced by the underlying asset. Therefore they are classified as derivatives. So, for example, if the share price goes up, the call option's value also increases and the put option decreases, and vice versa.

3.4 Call Option

If the stock goes up in price, the call option also values, and if the stock depreciates, so does the option. What drives people to buy options is the chance of a high return with a small initial investment.

Let's review the example from the beginning of the book, when the XYZ share spikes up, in scenario 3, in which Joseph was right, and the stock reached the value of $56.

Let's just look at the buyer Joseph. However, before we undertake the analysis, I must comment on something I have not yet mentioned:

In addition to exercising the option to buy the shares, Joseph can also sell the same option contract, which is now worth $400, to another person in the options market. The amount of $400 is the difference between the exercise price of $52 and the current value of the share, $56.

See below the previous example where Joseph exercises the right to buy and then right away sells the XYZ share in scenario 3, and the alternative of reselling the option contract on the market.

Exercise the right to buy:
Shares Market Value: $5,600
Right to buy: Joseph did exercise the right to buy at $52 per share
Bought for: $5.200
Sold for: $5.600
Gain: $400
(-) $200 premium
Profit: $200

Alternative: resell the option contract on the market:
Instead of exercising his right, Joseph now decides to sell the option contract on the market to somebody else. He initially bought the option to open the position; now, he can sell it on the market to close and get out of the trade.

Bought for: $200
Sells for $400
Profit: $200

In this situation, Joseph chooses to sell the same contract on the market to close it. He initially bought it for $200 and now sells it on the market for $400.

Note that when deciding not to exercise the right he has to buy, according to the terms of the option contract, Joseph also does not need to disburse the $5,200 to buy and sell the shares. As a result, he earned the same profit of $200 and pocketed only $200.

This is what attracts people to buy options: a high return with a small investment. But the stock has to rise considerably before the contract expires, causing the probability of profit for the buyer to be very low.

So once again, we choose to be like Ana and sell the covered call option rather than buying options.

3.5 Options Expiration Day

Unlike the shares of a company, where it is possible to keep them for life, as long as the company does not go bankrupt, options lose life (value) over time until they cease to exist and simply disappear.

Therefore, in this book, I teach the investor to be the option seller and take advantage of the fact that option value erodes over time.

The expiration day is the last day of life for the option. After that day, it ceases to exist and disappears entirely from the list of options on the stock exchange.

For the holder or buyer of the option, this is the last day to exercise the right to buy, in the case of the call, and the right to sell for the buyer in case of the put.

The standard stock options in the USA expires on the third Friday of each month.

❖ **Months of Expiration:** every month of the year.

❖ **Expiration day**: on the third Friday of each month. In the event of a holiday or for any other reason where the trading session is not open, the expiration is the third Thursday of the month.

❖ **Last trading day of the option contract**: In the USA you can trade options on the expiration date (Friday). However, in some countries, this might be different. The last trading session day might be the day before the expiry date.

You have to check the product you are trading because they may differ. For instance, the VIX and SPX index has different expiring times (am morning), which is different from the stock options. In addition, other assets might have different rules.

In Australia, the options on Australian equities expire every month but on the Thursday before the last business Friday of each month.

❖ **Months of Expiration**: every month of the year.

❖ **Expiration day**: Thursday before last Friday of each month.

❖ **Last trading day of the option contract:** the expiration day (Thursday) the day that the options contract expires.

Index options in Australia expire on the third Thursday of the month; please check the ASX website for updated details.

3.6 Standard Quantity

Options are traded only on contracts of at least 100 units, and each unit is equivalent to one share (asset). That is, to sell an option contract, you must have in your portfolio at least 100 shares of the underlying asset.

1 option contract = 100 shares

Number of contracts	Required number of shares
1	100
2	200
3	300

Table 1. Standard Quantity

Options are quoted in unit values; then, when an option is sold for $1, the contract's total value will be $100 (100 x $1). If, for example, you own 250 shares of Coca-Cola, you can sell two options contracts, which are equivalent to 200 shares. Thus, for every 100 quantities of an asset, you can sell an option contract.

3.7 Strike Price and Premium

The strike or exercise price is the price chosen by the seller and buyer in the option contract. The stock exchange offers several strike prices so that investors can adopt various strategies with options.

In the example where Ana owned 100 shares of XYZ, she acquired each for $50 and accepted a $2 option premium to sell the shares at the strike or exercise price of $52 to Joseph within a month.

Imagine the same scenario cited—the share price on the market is $50, the contract time also remains the same and expires in a month—but this time, Ana decides to change only the exercise price, from $52 to $60.

Would Joseph pay the same amount of $2 per share for the contract (premium)? Of course not; in this case, the exercise price is $60, the premium would be much lower, about $0.10 per share, because the chances of the asset going from $50 to $60 in a month are lower than from $50 to $52.

What if the exercise price was $48? With the stock at $50, this exercise price would have a much higher premium, maybe $3.50.

Simulation with the XYZ stock at $50

Strike Price	delta	Premium
$50	0.50	$3
$52	0.40	$2
$56	0.20	$1
$60	0.04	$0.10

Table 2. Strike or Exercise price and premium

The further away, the further out-of-the-money (OTM), the strike or exercise price of the call option is relative to the share price, the lower the option premium, because the farther away, the lower the chance or probability of this price being reached.

3.8 European Options vs. American

The above term does not refer to the geography from where options are traded. The United States, Europe and many other countries use both styles, which refer only to when the option can be exercised.

European-style options can only be exercised on the expiration date, which is better for the seller and worse for the buyer, because if the buyer decides to exercise the right to buy, they will have to wait until the last day of the option contract—that is, until the day of expiration. For example, if there are 40 days left until the end of the contract, the buyer has to wait until the last day to exercise the right to buy.

On the other hand, American-style options can be exercised from the next business day after their acquisition until the last day of expiration of the contract. If it is a 40-day contract, the buyer has virtually the entire contract period to decide.

However, in practice, this does not happen. Let's analyse the following example; the price paid for the option does not matter in this scenario.

If you purchased a call option that expires in 40 days, let's assume that the exercise price is $40 and, after ten days, the stock values and is quoted at $45.

In case you exercise the right to buy, you will earn $5 per option ($45 - $40), which is the difference between the asset price and the option strike price, which is the intrinsic value.

But, as there are still 30 days before expiration, this option contract would have a total value of $6.50. This is because the option is in-the-money (ITM) and has an intrinsic value of $5 and extrinsic of $1.50.

The extrinsic value is the same as time value or time, which in this example is 30 days. So if you exercise this option, it's like throwing the amount of $1.50 per share in the trash.

In this example, for the option buyer, it would be better to sell back this contract on the market for $6.50. For this reason, most options are exercised in the last week or on the last day, when most of the time value has already gone.

See below for more details on intrinsic and extrinsic value.

3.9 Intrinsic and Extrinsic Value

The total price or premium of an option is composed of the intrinsic and extrinsic value, which refer to the strike price in relation to the asset's value.

The intrinsic value is the tangible value of the option when time runs out, and the option expires. That is, it is the value that is in-the-money (ITM).

The extrinsic value refers to the time value. For example, the option that expires in two months is more expensive than the one that expires in a month because it has more time.

Volatility also influences the extrinsic value, as it represents the high or low demand for the referring option, which consequently affects the price.

If an option that expires today at this very moment still has some value, this is the intrinsic value because time is up. The intrinsic value is what is ITM. This means that when an option expires, it is only worth the value ITM.

If the option that expires at this very moment is worth nothing, it will turn to dust and disappear; this means that the exercise price is out-of-the-money (OTM).

Let's look at the following example in table 3 below, a stock priced at $30 and has the call options A and B, which expire in 30 days.

Let's look at these options from the beginning of the 30 days to the last day, expiring. To better explain this theoretical example, suppose the share price remains the same at $30 throughout the period.

Share value: $30
Duration of the option contract: 30 days

Option A - ITM In-the-Money					
Total value	Time remaining	Share price	Strike Price	Intrinsic Value	Extrinsic value
$3	30 days	$30	$28	$2	$1
$2.05	1 day	$30	$28	$2	$0.05
$2	zero	$30	$28	$2	$00

Option B - OTM Out-of-the-Money					
Total value	Time remaining	Share price	Strike Price	Intrinsic Value	Extrinsic value
$1	30 days	$30	$32	$00	$1
$0.05	1 day	$30	$32	$00	$0.05
$00	zero	$30	$32	$00	$00

Table 3. Intrinsic and Extrinsic Value

Option A – Strike Price $28

As I mentioned, options ITM have intrinsic value, which is calculated by the asset price minus the option strike price. This option strike price is $28, so it is ITM and has an intrinsic value of $2. This value is calculated by the share price minus the option's strike price ($30 - $28).

With 30 days until expiration, the option total value is $3, which is composed of the intrinsic value of $2, calculated above, and the remaining $1, which is the extrinsic value, referring to the remaining time of 30 days. Thus, after calculating the intrinsic value, the remaining value (what is left) is always the extrinsic value of time.

With one day to go, the total cost of the option is $2.05, composed of the intrinsic value of $2 and the remainder, which is the extrinsic amount of time of $0.05. With one day to expire, this time value is almost zero.

The next day, the option contract expired. As the share is $30 and the exercise price is $28, the total cost of option A on the market is $2, composed only of the intrinsic value.

Notice that the extrinsic value (time value) decreased day by day from $1 to $0.05 and disappeared or turned zero, leaving only the intrinsic value of $2.

Every option, when it expires, is worth only the intrinsic value: the extrinsic value decreases over time until it becomes zero.

Option B – Strike Price $32

As the share price is $30, the exercise price of $32 is OTM. OTM options have no intrinsic value, so the extrinsic value represents the total cost of the option. In this case, the extrinsic value is $1, which is the full price of this option.

With 30 days before expiration, the option is worth $1; one day before it expires, the value is $0.05, until it turns to dust after expiration and ceases to exist.

In the case of option B, on the last day before expiration, even OTM, it can still be worth a few cents, as in this example, $0.05. If volatility increases, the value of this option increases, and the price increase are not good for the seller.

But after expiration, if the share price remains below the exercise price of $32, the option will turn to dust anyway because all the time has expired, and this option has no intrinsic value.

As I mentioned earlier, the options only have some value at expiration if the exercise price is ITM. Therefore, for option B to have some value, the share price (underlying asset) should value and be above $32, which is the exercise or strike price of this option.

3.10   In-the-Money,   At-the-Money, and Out-of-the-Money

Other classification terms widely used in the options market are: in-the-money, at-the-money, and out-of-the-money. Some people might also use the term moneyness to classify an option.

The moneyness of an option is always related to the price of the underlying asset, which can be a stock, ETF, or index.

Moneyness of an option
In-The-Money (ITM)
At-The-Money (ATM)
Out-Of-The-Money (OTM)

❖ Call option: - In-The-Money (ITM). The strike or exercise price of the option is lower than the asset (share) price.

❖ Call option: - At-The-Money (ATM). The strike price of the option is equal to or close to the asset price.

❖ Call option: - Out-Of-The-Money (OTM). The strike price of the option is higher than the asset price.

See Figure 4, the options chain for Coca-Cola company KO, which, at the date of our analysis, June 11, 2021, was quoted at $55.65 per share. These options contracts expire on July 02, 2021, in about three weeks.

KO Option Chain

Date	Option	Calls & Puts	Moneyness
July 2021	Composite	Calls	Near the Money

	Calls						
Exp. Date	Last	Change	Bid	Ask	Volume	Open Int.	Strike
July 02, 2021							
Jul 02	--	--	5.10	5.30	--	--	50.50
Jul 02	--	--	4.40	4.75	--	--	51.00
Jul 02	4.19	--	4.10	4.55	2	--	51.50
Jul 02	4.02	--	3.50	3.75	--	6	52.00
Jul 02	3.65	--	3.10	3.35	--	3	52.50
Jul 02	3.19	--	2.60	2.85	--	10	53.00
Jul 02	2.07	-0.11 ▼	2.12	2.46	1	13	53.50
Jul 02	1.79	-0.39 ▼	1.69	1.97	11	19	54.00
Jul 02	1.42	-0.23 ▼	1.29	1.57	4	96	54.50
Jul 02	1.06	-0.23 ▼	0.96	1.03	61	987	55.00
Jul 02	0.75	-0.12 ▼	0.68	0.77	36	257	55.50
Jul 02	0.55	-0.07 ▼	0.48	0.53	33	305	56.00
Jul 02	0.39	-0.03 ▼	0.33	0.38	64	1338	56.50
Jul 02	0.27	-0.02 ▼	0.23	0.27	2723	3396	57.00
Jul 02	0.17	-0.03 ▼	0.16	0.19	5	292	57.50
Jul 02	0.12	-0.06 ▼	0.11	0.14	346	87	58.00
Jul 02	0.10	+0.01 ▲	0.08	0.10	10	16	58.50
Jul 02	0.07	--	0.06	0.09	1	44	59.00

Figure 3. Coca-Cola-KO at $55.65 (options chain).
Source: nasdaq.com

As the share value is at $55.65, we have the following classification for the options in Figure 3:

Among the various strike prices in the last column of the options chain, the strikes from $50.50 to $55.00 are below the share price; therefore, they are ITM.

Although the strike price of $55.50 is slightly below the share price of $55.65 and it is 0.15 cents ITM, it is classified as ATM because it is very close to the share price; therefore, the moneyness of the strike of $55.50 is ATM.

The strike prices of $56.00 and above this value are higher than the share price; so, they're OTM.

To exemplify what happens in real life, let's choose three options from Figure 3, one ITM, one ATM, and one OTM.

❖ July 02 - ITM - Strike $54.50

❖ July 02 - ATM - Strike $55

❖ July 02 - OTM – Strike $56

Suppose we are now on July 02, 2021, after the market closes and all those options have expired, and the KO share has devalued a little; the share price is now $55.00. That is what will happen to the following options:

Strike $54.50 - expired ITM because the strike price of $54.50 is lower than the share price. As the share is at $55, this option still has an intrinsic value of $0.50 ($55 - $54.50).

All the options below the strike price of $54.50 expired ITM; you can do the same calculation to find out each of these options value on the expiration day.

With the share at $55, any option with a strike equal to or above $55 will expire worthless. So, the other two options with the strike prices of $55 and $56 are OTM. As time passed, they expired and simply disappeared; they are worth nothing because there is no intrinsic value.

3.11 Selecting the Call to be Sold

It is important to remember again that the further away from the share price, the cheaper the call option will be because the underlying asset is less likely to reach that value OTM.

When implementing the strategy of selling the covered call, the investor has to choose the strike price, ITM, ATM, or OTM.

Selling an ITM call is a more conservative strategy because the premium coming from this strike price is of higher value, which helps to reduce the average cost of the stock and, consequently, reduces the loss in case of a fall in the asset price.

The calculations in the examples below will consider buying the shares for the current share price and simultaneously selling the call; if you already have the shares in your portfolio, you have to calculate the average costs of those shares.

When selling an ITM covered call, the investor might lose in the transaction of buying and selling the shares, as it is or may be sold for a value lower than the purchase price. But, on the other hand, it gains a high value in premium, which compensate for the loss in the stock.

ATM is a more moderate strategy. The option ATM is also the option that has the most extrinsic value. By selling the covered call using the ATM option, the profit is not earned by valuing the stock, as it will be sold for a price close to what was initially acquired.

OTM is a more optimistic and aggressive strategy—or, as they say in the business, more bullish. As the exercise price is OTM, the premium paid is lower, which offers less protection in case of a fall in the price of the asset because the reduction in the average share cost is lower.

However, when the stock rises, the strategy profits with the appreciation of the stock and also with the premium received from the sale of the option. All of this, of course, is if the share goes up.

The strategy of selling options OTM is for the investor who is optimistic and anticipates the stock's appreciation, whether based on fundamental analysis, technical analysis, or the recommendation of research firms.

Figure 4 below shows the option chain for Procter & Gamble, code PG. Data accessed on June 10, 2021, and the share price on that day was $134.79. The options selected expire on July 16, 2021.

For this example, we selected three options;

- ❖ Strike 130 - ITM (in-the-money)
- ❖ Strike 135 - ATM (at-the-money)
- ❖ Strike 140 - OTM (out-of-money)

PG		PROCTER & GAMBLE CO COM	**134.79**		ETB NYSE	±0.623	

Underlying

	Last X	Net Chng	Bid X	Ask X	Size	Volum
>	134.79 N	-.05	134.65 P	134.90 P	3 x 2	6,200,78

> Trade Grid

Option Chain Days to exp.: **32 - max** Spread: **Single** Layout: **Delta, Gamma, Theta, Vega**

				CALLS			Strikes: 10	
	Delta	Gamma	Theta	Vega	Bid X	Ask X	Exp	Strike
16 JUL 21	(37) 100							
	.94	.00	-.02	.05	24.40 N	25.55 P	16 JUL 21	110
	.93	.01	-.02	.05	19.25 P	20.75 N	16 JUL 21	115
	.92	.01	-.02	.06	14.70 X	15.40 Z	16 JUL 21	120
	.86	.03	-.02	.10	10.05 X	10.60 X	16 JUL 21	125
	.73	.04	-.03	.14	5.65 Q	6.10 X	16 JUL 21	130
	.48	.06	-.03	.17	2.52 B	2.60 B	16 JUL 21	135
	.21	.04	-.02	.13	.76 Z	.79 B	16 JUL 21	140
	.07	.02	-.01	.06	.21 Z	.24 X	16 JUL 21	145
	.03	.01	-.01	.03	.08 Z	.10 Z	16 JUL 21	150
	.02	.00	.00	.02	.04 Z	.06 Z	16 JUL 21	155

Figure 4. PG Options Chain.
Source: Thinkorswim platform

3.11.1   In-The-Money (ITM)

Let's do an analysis simulating the sale of an ITM option when implementing the covered call strategy.

Share price: $134.79
Strike price: $130

If you buy 100 shares of Procter & Gamble (PG) at $134.79 per share and choose to sell the call option with the strike price of $130 (data from Figure 4), you will receive for this sale the amount of $5.65 (ask column) or $565, equivalent to 100 shares.

Note that the option is ITM because the strike price is lower than the stock value.

Stock increases — Maximum profit

If, for instance, on the expiration day of the option contract, the share has increased from $134.79 to $142, you will not profit anything from this price increase.

In fact, you will lose because the owner of the option will exercise the right to buy it from you. Then you receive an assignment notification and will have to sell your shares for $130 each, a price lower than the price you paid, $134.79.

This will happen if, on the expiration day, the share price is at least one cent above the $130 price. So, this will have a high probability of happening when selling ITM calls.

Notice that you, the investor, lose in the asset sale (-) $479 because the share was bought for $134.79 and sold for $130, which is the exercise or strike price. But the premium you received, of $565, is the largest among the three options listed in Figure 4 because this option is ITM. The final result is a positive balance of $0.86 per share (maximum profit) or $186 for 100 shares.

You can see that the high premium you received offset the loss in the stock, and you still have a profit at the end of the transaction.

Stock decreases - Breakeven point

On the other hand, if, at the expiration of the option, the stock suffers a big price fall and is quoted at or below the strike price ($130), the option buyer will not exercise their right to buy the stock because it is cheaper on the market. As a result, this option will expire worthless.

Consequently, you will have to keep the shares that are now at the value of $130; you always keep the premium received—in this case, $565.

The breakeven point is the amount paid for the share minus the premium received from the sale of the option. Therefore, $134.79 minus the $5.65 means that if the stock falls to $129.14, a drop of more than almost 4%, you will not lose any of your initial investment.

The above math was done in unit values. Multiplying everything by 100, we will have the total initial amount invested of $13,479, which, with the devaluation of the stock to $129.14, became $12,914. As you keep the premium of $565, the total equity is again worth $13,479 ($12,914 + $565).

Selling the covered call ITM is like buying insurance that was paid by someone else—the buyer of the call. The only negative factor is that this strategy eliminates the earning potential when the stock rises.

Stock decreases (equilibrium point)
$129.14

Stock increases (maximum profit)
$0.86 per share or $86

ITM — Advantages

- ❖ Increased protection in the event of a fall in the price of the asset

- ❖ Further reduction in the average cost price of the asset

ITM — Disadvantages

- ❖ Lower return when the stock rises

- ❖ The investor loses in the asset sale when there is an assignment (the option buyer exercises the right to buy).

3.11.2   Out-Of-the-Money (OTM)

Now, let's analyze the sale of the OTM option, given in Figure 4.

Share price: $134.79

Strike price: $140

Say you buy the 100 shares of 3M for $134.79 each and, this time, choose to sell the call with the exercise or strike price of $140. In this case, you will sell an OTM option because the strike price is higher than the value of the stock.

Stock increases — Maximum profit

You will receive for this sale a premium of $0.76. If, on the expiration day of the option contract, the share has increased in value, from $134.79 to $141, for instance, you will now profit from the appreciation and also from the premium received.

This is because the owner of the option will exercise the right to buy and you will have to sell the shares for $140 each.

Therefore, as you paid $134.79 per share and will have a unit profit on the sale of (+) $5.21, in addition to the premium you received of $0.76, then you will close the transaction with a total profit of $5.97 per share or $597 for 100 shares.

The $0.76 premium received consists of 100% extrinsic value (time) and zero intrinsic value because the exercise price was OTM.

Stock decreases — Breakeven point

If at expiration, the stock stays at or below $140, which is the strike price, this option will expire worthless, and you will keep the shares and the total value of the premium $0.76.

In the case of a decline in the stock price, again, the breakeven point is the amount paid for the stock minus the premium received by the option; therefore, $134.79 minus $0.76 equals $134.03. This means that if the stock depreciates to $134.03, you will not lose anything of your initial investment.

Stock decreases — Breakeven point
$134.03

Stock increases — Maximum profit
$5.97 per share or $597

OTM - Advantages

❖ This strategy profits with the appreciation of the stock and with the premium received

❖ It is less likely to be exercised; that is, there is a greater probability of keeping your shares while receiving the premium.

OTM — Disadvantages

❖ Less protection

❖ The premium received is lower.

3.11.3   In the Money vs. Out of the Money

Let's compare the two options:

In the money - ITM
Exercise or strike price (option): $130
Share price: $134.79
Breakeven Point: $129.14
Maximum Profit: $0.86

Out of the money - OTM
Exercise or strike price (option): $140
Share price: $134.79
Breakeven Point: $134.03
Maximum Profit: $5.97

If the stock price falls, the breakeven point with the ITM option is greater. Supposing the stock depreciates to $129.14, there are no losses on the initial investment; therefore, ITM is a more defensive strategy.

The OTM option has a lower breakeven point of $134.03. If the stock falls below this price, there will be losses.

In the case of appreciation, the OTM option is better because the total gain of $5.97 per share is higher and refers to the stock's appreciation price with the addition of the premium.

However, for the ITM option, in the case of an increase in the stock price, the maximum profit is $0.86 (unit value).

When choosing the strike price, it will depend on how you feel about the asset. If it's a stock you want to keep in your portfolio, maybe an OTM option is the best choice.

If you are not very optimistic, it may be better to sell the call ITM because it will give you greater protection in case of a fall in price.

3.12   The Greeks

The Greeks refer to the Greek letters, except for vega, which is not a Greek letter but is still part of the Greeks metric.

They are used to price and understand the scale of options risk. The most commonly used Greeks are delta, theta, and vega, which will be discussed below. There are also gamma and rho, which will be mentioned at the end of the book.

In addition to the strike price, time to expiration and volatility are the primary agents that influence the options price. Other less important factors are interest rate and dividends.

The Greeks influence the options price, but we must not forget that the underlying asset's price is also an important factor in pricing.

Asset Price (share)	Call Option Price
Share price increases	Call value increases
Share price decreases	Call value decreases

Table 4. Share Price vs. Call Option Price.

3.12.1   Delta

Delta (Δ), in addition to other functions, measures the chance of an option reaching the exercise price and being worth at least one cent by the expiration date of the option.

For example, a delta of 0.10 means that the option has a probability close to 10% of ending in the money until expiration, while 0.20 means 20%, and so on.

Table 5 below shows that the further or more OTM the option is, the smaller is the delta and the lower the chance of the underlying asset reaching that strike price before the option expires.

You can see that the chance of the strike price of $60 worth at least one cent before the option's expiration is 4%. One can also read this backwards and say that this option has a 96% chance of expiring without value by the end of the 30 days.

Delta also measures the rate at which the option price can change relative to the change in the asset price. For example, an option with a delta of 0.50 means that if the stock increases $1, the option price will increase by approximately $0.50. Likewise, if the delta is 0.40 and the stock increased by $1, the option price would increase by $0.40, and so on.

Company XYZ: $50 per share
Option expiration: 30 days

Strike Price	Delta	Premium
$50	0.50	$3.00
$52	0.40	$2.00
$56	0.20	$1.00
$60	0.04	$0.10

Table 5. Delta

3.12.2   Vega and Volatility

Vega is a metric that indicates how the option price will be affected by each increase or decrease in volatility.

The important thing to understand here is that volatility increases when there is a high demand for options and decreases with the fall in demand.

Volatility	Option value
Increases	Increases
Decreases	Decreases

Table 6. Vega and Volatility

Volatility is the sharp variation in the demand of options for both the call and the put option; that is, the law of supply and demand from options buyers and sellers.

This is influenced by an environment of pessimism or optimism, such as those causes by the dates of the company's earnings results, news (short period), wars, and political events. In the case of optimism, demand for the call option increases because this option is used to speculate on a possible rise in the underlying assets (shares, index, or ETF).

In the case of pessimism, the demand for put options increases. The put is like insurance against the devaluation of an asset, and fearful investors pay for that insurance to avoid losses.

Some speculators buy both puts and calls to speculate on the rise or fall in the stock price due to events like a company's earnings announcement.

In practice, during these events, the price of options (call and put) can triple or quadruple: this is high implied volatility. However, after these events, the demand for options decreases and, with this, volatility also decreases along with the option price.

3.12.3   Theta (Time)

Theta is a negative number that represents, in theory, the expected value at which the option will depreciate during a single day.

Imagine an option OTM that expires in 30 days. Now imagine, theoretically, that the 30 days have passed and that the underlying share remains at the same value.

This means that the option has expired OTM, with no value, as we saw in the intrinsic value and extrinsic value section.

The theta number shows how much this option loses value each day. For example, a theta of -0.20 means that the option will lose the value of $0.20 each day, theoretically, if the asset does not change the price until expiration.

In the following options A and B, see the value these options lose after a single day. This amount or decline of the option value refers to theta.

Option A
Option price today: $2.50
Theta: -0.30
Option price after one day: $2.20

Option B
Option price today: $1.20
Theta: -0.05
Option price after one day: $1.15

It is worth remembering that theta (time) is a friend of the options seller. When you sell an option, theta becomes positive. The more time that passes, the more the option loses value, and then you can repurchase it cheaper.

For the option buyer, theta is the enemy. When you buy an option, time starts running against you until the option turns to dust and expires worthless. If the underlying asset does not move in the direction you predicted, all the money invested will be lost; so, the buyer has a negative theta.

3.12.4   Time Decay

Theta is not a fixed or linear value known as theta decay, time decay, or corrosion of the extrinsic value (time). It shows how the value of an option slowly decreases or erodes as time passes.

Still, the corrosion of value increases as time passes and so increases the theta number until it begins to accelerate (increase faster) as the option is near expiration. In the last 20 days, the theta increases significantly, and the option value starts to plummet.

For example, Option A shown earlier has theta -0.30, which causes the option to lose $0.30 per day, theoretically, if the stock does not change the price. After a week, theta can increase to -0.40, and the option will be losing $0.40 per day. After one month, theta may be worth -0.70, which causes the option to devalue $0.70 per day.

This means that the theta increases with the passage of time, which makes the price of the option depreciate faster. It is worth remembering that options deep ITM have little extrinsic value, and theta does not affect them much. Theta significantly affects the options ATM.

Notice in Figure 5 that from 120 to 90 days, after 30 days, the price of the option fell only $5 ($300 to $295), and that from 90 to 60 days, after another 30 days, the price declined at a much higher rate of $10 ($295 to $285).

The shorter the time remaining until the option expires, the greater is the theta and the daily reduction in the option price. From 45 to 30 days, the option price declines by $50.

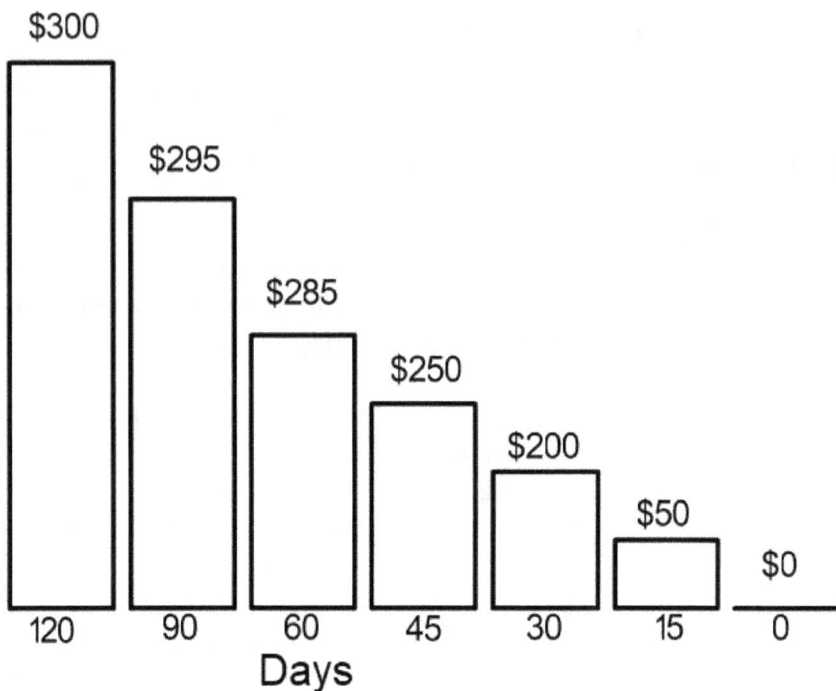

Figure 5. Days remaining time vs. Declining of the option value

This example is just a visual illustration to better understand the time decay or corrosion of the option's value relative to time.

The following graph, Figure 6, from the My Journey to Millions website, shows theta or time decay and the corrosion of the value of the options in relation to time.

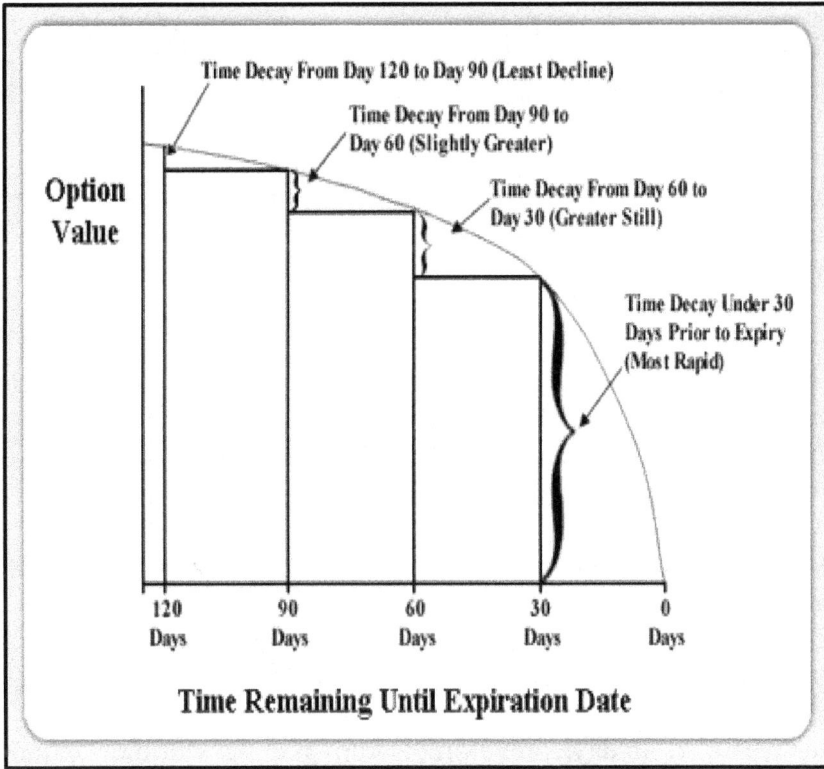

Figure 6. MYJOURNEYTOMILLIONS.COM/ARTICLES/TIME-DECAY-LOVE/

The days on the y-axis, in Figure 6, refer to the remaining time until the options expire; the curve forming an arc relates to the option's value.

Notice that the curve declines from 120 days to 60 days. With 30 days left, theta increases greatly, and the value of the options begins to plummet faster.

3.13 Choosing the Expiration Date

If we hire car insurance, we know that the longer we hire this service, the higher the price we will pay for it. So, for example, three-month insurance is more costly than two-month insurance.

In the options market, the same applies. For instance, if we sell a call that expires in three months, even though we receive a good premium, we will give the buyer a lot of time; our asset will also be tied to this option for a long time. But if we sell the option that expires in a week, the premium is very low and not worth the investment.

Based on the previous Figure 6 and numerous studies, such as research by Tastytrade's team, entitled "Why 45 days before it expires is the magic number?", it is recommended to sell options with 45 days remaining until expiration.

The period of 45 days remaining is known in the world of options as the "sweet spot" for the seller. This is because the value of the option in relation to the time is still high and will soon begin into decay very quickly—and we should take advantage of that because we have the opportunity to sell something at a reasonable price, which will soon lose value and can be repurchased much cheaper.

It doesn't have to be a fixed number, but it's good to choose a number close to 45 days before expiration: it can be between 60 and 30 days.

Of course, this is just one of the (theoretical) components that calculate how options are priced. However, it provides us with a guide, such as an instruction manual to operate with the numbers in our favor.

3.14 Codes Used on the Stock Exchange

Some brokers facilitate the operational process, and there is no need to memorize the codes below. But it is essential to understand the option codes or tickers that you are planning to trade.

These codes are composed of first the ticker code of the underlying security (stock, ETF, or index), the expiration (year, month, and day), the strike price, a call or put, and lastly, the strike price of the option.

They are given in the following order: (ticker symbol) + Expiration Year (yy) + Expiration Month (mm) + Expiration Day (dd) + Call/Put Indicator (C or P) + Strike Price:

Symbol (max. 6 characters)
Yr (YY)
Mo (MM)
Day (DD)
Call or Put (C/P)
Strike Price (#####.###) listed with three or five digits before the decimal and three digits following the decimal.

For example, a June 11, 2021 strike $54.00 Call Option on Coca-Cola would be listed as "KO 210611C00054000."

3.15 How to Read the Options Chain

Let's use all the information we've learned so far to understand the options chain. The options chain lists calls and puts with multiple strikes that are the exercise prices, referring to the underlying asset, which could be stocks, indices, or ETFs.

It is essential to familiarize yourself with the options chain so that, as an investor, you can choose the best option to sell, one that offers a reasonable premium in relation to the time of the contract.

Some brokers provide this information on their own platform. You can also go to sites like Yahoo Finance or Nasdaq.com, and in Australia, the ASX website, to find all of this information for free—although probably not in real-time.

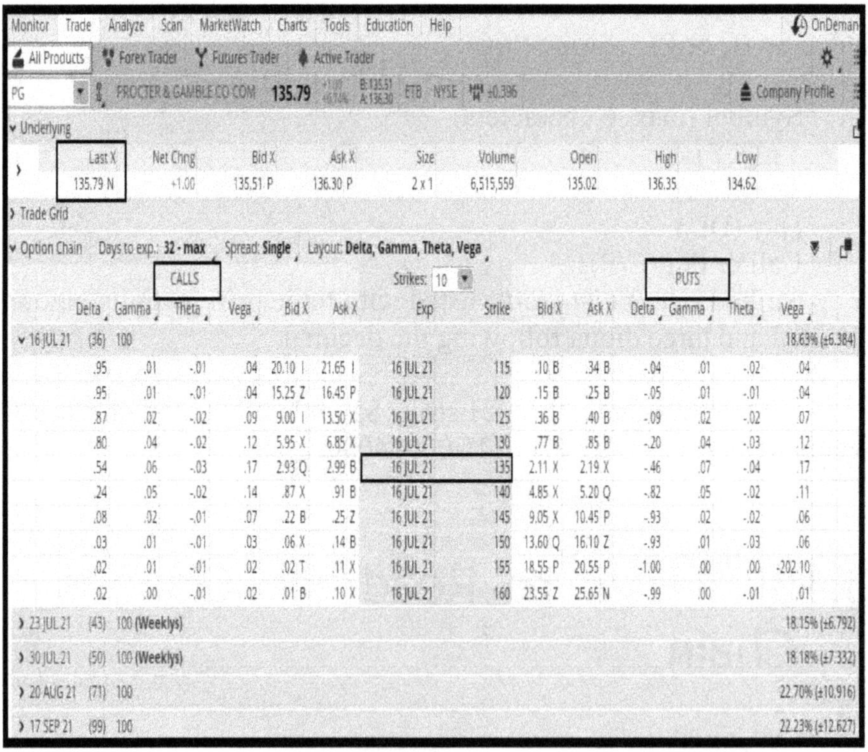

Last X	Net Chng	Bid X	Ask X	Size	Volume	Open	High	Low
135.79 N	+1.00	135.51 P	136.30 P	2 x 1	6,515,559	135.02	136.35	134.62

Delta	Gamma	Theta	Vega	Bid X	Ask X	Exp	Strike	Bid X	Ask X	Delta	Gamma	Theta	Vega
16 JUL 21 (36) 100													18.63% (±6.384)
.95	.01	-.01	.04	20.10 I	21.65 I	16 JUL 21	115	.10 B	.34 B	-.04	.01	-.02	.04
.95	.01	-.01	.04	15.25 Z	16.45 P	16 JUL 21	120	.15 B	.25 B	-.05	.01	-.01	.04
.87	.02	-.02	.09	9.00 I	13.50 X	16 JUL 21	125	.36 B	.40 B	-.09	.02	-.02	.07
.80	.04	-.02	.12	5.95 X	6.85 X	16 JUL 21	130	.77 B	.85 B	-.20	.04	-.03	.12
.54	.06	-.03	.17	2.93 Q	2.99 B	16 JUL 21	135	2.11 X	2.19 X	-.46	.07	-.04	.17
.24	.05	-.02	.14	.87 X	.91 B	16 JUL 21	140	4.85 X	5.20 Q	-.82	.05	-.02	.11
.08	.02	-.01	.07	.22 B	.25 Z	16 JUL 21	145	9.05 X	10.45 P	-.93	.02	-.02	.06
.03	.01	-.01	.03	.06 X	.14 B	16 JUL 21	150	13.60 Q	16.10 Z	-.93	.01	-.03	.06
.02	.01	-.01	.02	.02 T	.11 X	16 JUL 21	155	18.55 P	20.55 P	-1.00	.00	.00	-202.10
.02	.00	-.01	.02	.01 B	.10 X	16 JUL 21	160	23.55 Z	25.65 N	-.99	.00	-.01	.01
23 JUL 21 (43) 100 (Weeklys)													18.15% (±6.792)
30 JUL 21 (50) 100 (Weeklys)													18.18% (±7.332)
20 AUG 21 (71) 100													22.70% (±10.916)
17 SEP 21 (99) 100													22.23% (±12.627)

Figure 7.Option Chain PG. Source: Thinkorswim Platform

At the top left of Figure 7 is the ticker for the underlying asset, in this case, Procter & Gamble, code PG, and the share price of $135.79, plus some information regarding the underlying asset.

Below we have the options chain for PG: on the left side are the call options, and on the right, the put options are listed. From Figure 7, we can see:

❖ The middle column lists all the strike prices for calls and puts with strikes from 115 to 160.

❖ ITM - in-the-money for the call options. Notice that the strikes from $155 to $135 are below the share price of $135.79. That's why these options are ITM.

❖ OTM - out-of-the-money for the call options. The rest of the options from strike $140 to $160 higher than the share price. So, they're OTM.

❖ Bid x Ask price - these are the option prices or premium—the bid price from option buyers and ask price from option sellers.

❖ In addition, it is also possible to view the volatility and delta, gamma, Theta, and Vega of all options.

Blank Page

4

Implementing the Covered Selling Strategy

As I mentioned earlier, if your sentiment toward the financial market and the assets on your portfolio is very optimistic, and if a high stock appreciation is expected, maybe this is not the best environment to sell the covered call. In this scenario, you can expect this appreciation and, after that occurs, start thinking about executing the strategy.

But if the market has already reached a peak high, is stagnant or moving sideways, or if you have a target price to sell some of your assets, the sale of the covered call is an excellent strategy.

While other investors see no positive results, the call seller will continue to profit in any environment on the market.

Again, it is worth remembering that the more out-of-the-money (OTM), the cheaper the call option will be because the further the exercise price, the lower the chance of the asset reaching that value.

To sell the call option, you must have the shares in the portfolio. Then, the two situations below can occur.

Holding a long position of the stock and then selling the call.
Imagine that the investor already has a portfolio with 300 shares of the Coca-Cola company and decides to sell the covered call. In this case, it is possible to sell three options contracts, as each contract is equivalent to 100 shares.

Simultaneously purchasing of the stock and selling the call.
If the investor does not own the assets, they must first buy the shares and then sell the call. Once the stock or asset purchase is confirmed, the investor can then execute the sale of the option.

Some brokers may facilitate this procedure. For example, the person interested in this type of operation can buy 100 shares at $30 each, for a total of $3,000, and sell the option for a unit value of $1, a total $100. These two transactions can be done in a single procedure, for a debit of $2,900, excluding commissions.

Depending on the brokerage you use, you might have to make these transactions in two separate procedures.

Never sell the call first without having the shares in the portfolio because this is characterized as naked selling, a strategy with much more risk.

4.1 Covered Call OTM – Out-of-the-money

To demonstrate in practice the implementation of the strategy, I chose as an example SPY ETF, which tracks the performance of the S&P500 index and, in this scenario, selling an option out of money.

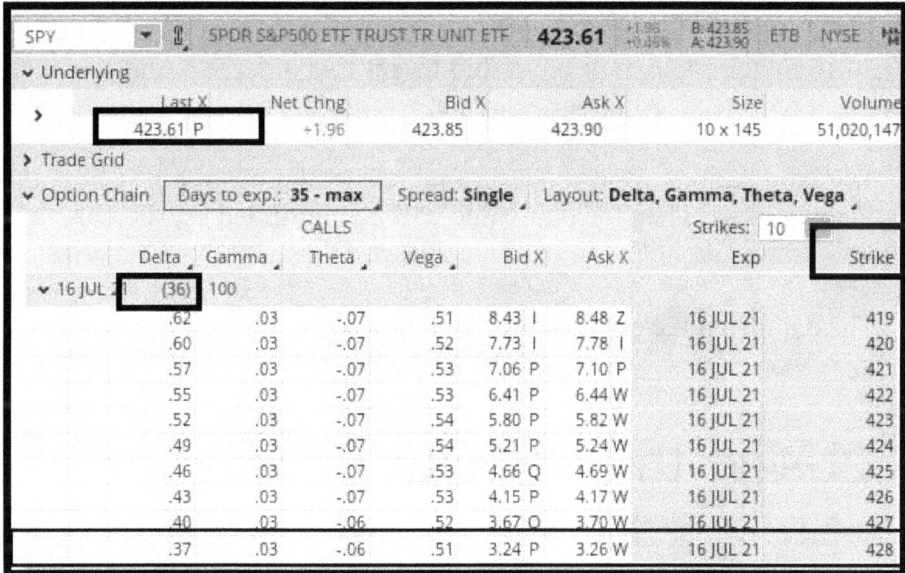

Figure 9. SPY options chain. Source: thinkorswim platform

See, in Figure 9, that the strike of the call option chosen to be sold was $428, an OTM strike price. Access date June 11, 2021

❖ Underlying ETF/Share price on the date of access: $423.61

❖ Strike/strike price: $428 OTM

❖ Delta: 0.37

❖ Option expiration date: July 16,2021

❖ Time: 36 calendar days

❖ Premium received: $3.24 per unit.

We sellers are asking the price we want ($3.26) to sell the option in the ask collum in Figure 9. Imagine we dropped the price from $3.26 to $3.24 to match the option buyer bid to get this order. So, the premium received will be $3.24 in our example.

The calculations were made in unit values because this is how the option is quoted. Then the unit value will be multiplied by 100, which is the minimum amount of an option contract equivalent to 100 shares.

The data from the above option will be used in the coming examples.

4.2 Using the Delta to Choose the Strike Price

As I explained earlier, delta has several functions, and one of them is that it can be used as a probability indicator.

I usually use the delta close to 0.30 or 30% because the option is OTM and still has a reasonable premium.

In Figure 9 before, the delta of the option is 0.37. Note that in the same line, this delta is tied to the chosen strike price of $428. It means that the probability of the stock reaching this price, up to the expiration date, is around 37% because of the delta of 0.37.

One can say that the probability of the option not reaching this strike price and turning to dust is around 61%, the opposite.

Using delta provides you with all this information before you execute the strategy.

It is clear that with one or even ten operations, the probability is inaccurate, but as the number of occurrences increases, the probability begins to work.

The use of delta is only an indicator. For example, you could also set a minimum value to sell options and use it as a reference.

4.3 Selling Calls on Stocks that you Already Hold

Imagine that you already have in your portfolio 100 SPY shares, which were purchased a few months ago, for the price of $350 per unit.

On today's date, you decide to sell a call option. Since you already have the shares in the portfolio, this strategy is called covered call or covered call writing.

With information on the options already available, as presented in the previous figure, you can implement the strategy.

The share price today is $423.61, as shown in previous Figure 9. If you like the idea of selling your shares for an even higher value than today and still receive a premium for it, then you are satisfied with the previous strike price of $428, which is OTM and pays a premium of $3.24 unit value.

According to the seller's obligation in the option contract, the strike chosen is the price you will have to sell your shares.

Below are the details of the operation:

❖ The initial purchase of 100 shares: Total $35,000

❖ Sale of call for $3.24: Total $324 (one contract)

❖ Strike price: $428

❖ Time remaining until the option contract expiration: 36 days

❖ Total cost of shares reduced to: $34,676 or $346.76 per unit

By buying the shares only, the total cost is $35,000. As you sold the option, you will receive a credit of $324 for this transaction. Thus, $34,676 becomes the total amount invested, which decreases the initial cost of the investment.

4.4 Wait Until the Expire Date

If you decide to wait until the expiration, you will receive the total amount of $324, referring to the premium. But the final result will depend on what happened to the asset, whether it went up in price or down.

Asset increases

If at the end of the option contract, which is 36 days, the SPY closes at any value above the strike price, you will receive an assignment notification from your broker and will have to sell your shares at this price, which is $428.

It does not matter if the stock closed at the price of $428 or $500. You will have to sell them for $428 and will also keep the premium of $324. In this case, this would be the result:

Initial purchase: $35,000
Final sale: $42,800

Profit: $7,800
Premium received: $324
Total profit: $8,124

Asset decreases

If, at the end of the 36 days, the share price is equal to or below the exercise price of $428, the option expires worthless. In this situation, you retain the stock in your portfolio and keep the premium of $324, generating a return of 0.92% in just 36 days.

This calculation is done by dividing the premium amount of $324 by the initial investment of $35,000 and then multiplying by 100 to reach the percentage.

If you can repeat such an operation ten times a year, you will get a return of 9.2% per year.

Remember that for each option contract sold, you must have 100 shares in the portfolio. Then, with two hundred shares, you could sell two contracts and collect $648 in premium. With three hundred shares in the portfolio, you could sell three contracts and collect $972 in premium, and so on.

Receiving the premium is like you're getting paid for owning assets.

4.5 Simultaneous Operation: Buy the Stocks and Sell the Call

We will use the same data from the previous example with the OTM option. The only difference in this scenario is that you will buy the shares at the current market price.

This example will be used until the end of the chapter, implementing the strategy.

In this case, you do not have the shares in the portfolio; therefore, you make a simultaneous transaction, which is to buy 100 shares of SPY for the current unit value of $423.61 and, at the same time or soon after, sell the option.

❖ Purchase of 100 shares: Total $42,361

❖ Sale of call for $3.24: Total $324 (one contract)

❖ Strike price: $428
❖ Time remaining until the option contract expiration: 36 days

❖ Total cost of shares reduced to: $42,037

If you only buy the shares, the total cost would be $42,361, but with the sale of the option, the premium of $324 is credited to your account. Then, the total cost of the investment decreases to $42,037. Therefore, you can also say that the unit cost of the shares decreased from $423.61 to $420.37.

4.6 Waiting until the Expiration Date

As I explained earlier, after expiration, the result will depend on what happened to the asset; that is, whether it valued or devalued.

Asset increases

If the stock closes at any price above $428 (it can be $428.01), you will receive an assignment notification and will have to sell them for $428, which is the exercise or strike price, as this is the seller's obligation.

In this case, you (seller) gain with the asset's appreciation because you chose an exercise price OTM and still get the premium of the option sold.

The transfer of your shares (assignment) to the person holding the option is done automatically by the broker. See the transaction result below:

Initial cost of buying the shares: $42,361
Final sale value of the shares: $42,800
Profit: $439
Premium received: $324
Total profit: $763
Return in just 36 days: 1.8% that includes the premium and the asset valuation.

Some people might do this math a bit differently by dividing the profit from the shares $439 at the end of the trade by the initial cost of the shares minus the premium ($439/$42,037). This way, the return will be slightly lower.

Devaluation of the asset

If the stock closes at $428, which is the strike price, or closes at any lower value, the option expires OTM (worthless), you will keep the shares and still retain the total amount of the premium, of $324, which will give you a return approximately of 0.76% in just 36 days.

In addition, you can still sell another option in the next cycle or in the next month of expiration.

4.7 Breakeven Point

In addition to reducing the cost of the shares, note that the sale of the option also provides protection in case of a decline in the asset price.

The break-even point is nothing more than when, in a given situation related to the stock market, a stock depreciates, and yet the investor does not lose money. In this case, it is the price paid per share minus the premium received from the sale of the option ($423.61-$3.24).

So, the break-even point in this example is $420.76 per share. If, at the expiration of the option, the stock price declines to this price, you do not lose anything from the initial investment because the call will expire without value, and you will get the premium of $324.

For the investor who bought the stock for $423.61 and did not opt for the option, every cent that the stock devalues will be lost.

4.8 Closing the Option Contract with 50% Profit

After starting the transaction, the investor can wait until expiration, as was seen earlier. But there is also the possibility to buy the option back and completely exit the option contract.

One of the advantages of selling the call in the shares you own is that if the stock depreciates, the call also devalues, and you can repurchase it cheaper. In this way, you are gaining from the devaluation of your asset.

We'll continue with the example of the concurrent operation and repeat the data below:

❖ Purchase of 100 shares: Total $42,361

❖ Sale of call for $3.24: Total $324 (one contract)

❖ Strike price: $428

❖ Time remaining until the option contract expiration: 36 days

❖ Total cost of shares reduced to: $42,037

Let's see how this works by closing the option before the expiration date and with a 50% profit if the stock price declines.

Next, Table 8 shows the type of transaction that should be performed on your online broker to start and exit the option trade, both for sellers and buyers. But remember that when selling the covered call explained in this book, you are the seller.

Transaction	Option seller	Option buyer
Start (open)	Sell for a credit	Buy for a debit
Finish (close)	Buy for a debit	Sell for a credit

Table 8. Open to enter and close to exit

Therefore, as a seller, you initially sell the option for a credit to start the trade and have to buy it back for a debit to exit the position (close). To profit, you should repurchase it cheaper than you sold.

One interesting strategy is to close the option with 50% profit and keep the shares if you consider it to be a good stock that you would like to keep in your portfolio, so you can continue selling the covered call for your shares.

Going back to the start of the transaction, you sold the option for a total credit of $324, and now, instead of waiting until expiration, you will repurchase the option at half of the price initially sold.

When the call is sold at the beginning of the transaction, the total credit received will appear on your online broker as follows: (-) $324. The negative amounts refer to the amount you will have to pay to exit the option before expiration and so you don't have to sell your shares.

As time goes by, and if the stock price does not rise, this value decreases with the time decay. See the simulation below:

(-) $324
(-) $300
(-) $280
(-) $190
(-) $162

After the initial sale of the option for a credit of $324, you can place an order to repurchase it (close it) for a debit of $162 and wait. When this order is executed, after a few days or weeks, you will completely exit the option position. You will again have the shares in the portfolio free and without any obligation attached to it.

To summarize the process, you initially received a credit of $324 for the sale of the call and had a debit of $162 when you repurchased the same option to close it and exit the trade, obtaining a profit of $162. The return is 0.38% ($162 / $42,361), calculated by the final profit, divided by the total amount initially invested.

When exiting the position with 50% profit, it is not necessary to wait until expiration. Therefore, the average time with the trade open can be only a few days if the asset depreciates fast or a few weeks.

Imagine if you could repeat this process once a month. Therefore, 0.38 x 12= 4.56% per year. If you can do it twice a month, you will have a return of approximately 9.12% per year. It's a remarkable increase in your income as if it were a dividend.

The sale of the covered call option is zero risk regarding the option because the risk remains in the asset, not in the option. As we have seen, the sale of the call helps to reduce the risks, as it decreases the average cost of the shares.

4.9 Rolling Forward When the Underlying Share Price Increases

We just saw how the time decay or corrosion of value happens. If the stock price does not increase too much, the option loses value, making it possible to repurchase it cheaper.

We also saw that after the sale of the option, the credit received appears in the brokerage account as a negative number because it refers to the amount you will have to pay to exit the option contract before the expiration date.

(-) $324
(-) $300
(-) $280
(-) $190
(-) $162

But if the stock price goes up considerably, the value of the option also goes up. If the option is now quoted at $424, this is the amount you will have to pay to exit the trade without having to wait until expiration. In this case, you would have a loss because it was sold for $324 and was bought back at a higher price for $400. See below.

(-) $324
(-) $424
(-) $480
(-) $500

Don't worry: options values are rising because your underlying stocks or assets, which you own, are also going up in price. That is why this operation is known as the covered call. When the option contract expires, and if the share value is above the option's exercise price, you will sell the shares at the strike price and still keep the premium, as I explained earlier, in "1.6 Wait until the Expiration Date".

The person who sold the naked option without having the stock in the portfolio would be very concerned about this price hike, but this is not the case for you. You would only lose, in this scenario, if you want to exit the option contract without waiting until expiration.

However, if this happens, the option value increases, and you want to get out before the expiration date, there is an alternative to this situation.

Now, let's look at the rolling techniques. At first, this technique may seem like a complicated topic. I suggest that after reading this book, you return to this part of the text after a few days or weeks. With time and some practice, you will assimilate everything that has been explained in this book.

Rolling is when the investor exits one option position and immediately starts another, using the same underlying asset and the same option type, in this case, the call.

The phrase "roll forward" means to close the current position and start another one the following month to add more premium in the trade because the longer the option contract is, the higher the value of the option.

Let's go back to the example at the beginning of this chapter. You initially sold the option with a strike price of $428 that expires in 36 days, July 16, 2021. The credit received was $3.24 unit value, a total of $324, referring to the 100 shares.

If the stock price keeps going up during the option contract period and is quoted above $428, which is the strike price, it is probably not possible to close the option with 50% profit. In this case, you do not want to wait until expiration, as I explained earlier.

Imagine that the stock is now worth $435 and, therefore, has passed the exercise price, and the sold option is now in-the-money (ITM); the same option you sold for $3.24 should now be worth about $4.24.
If you decide to repurchase the option to close the transaction and do not have to sell the stock, you will lose $1.00 unit value in the option.

However, remember that the longer the option contract duration is, the higher the option value. The options on the following month, in August 2021, with the same strike price of $428 or close to it, which is now ITM, should be worth about $5.74 or more.

Then, you close the initial trade and realize a loss of $1.00 and right after sell the August option, at the same exercise price, for $5.00. See what the situation looks like now:

Price per option initially sold: $3.24 credit
Price paid to close this position: $4.24 debit
Sale of the new option in August: $5.00 credit.

After realizing the loss of -$1, you sold the August option for $5.00. The remaining credit is $4.00 or $400 when multiplied by 100 shares. You added another 30 days to the operation, and now the whole cycle repeats itself.

If the stock comes to depreciate, you can try to buy back the last option sold for a lower price and close the option position. Always calculate all the debits and credits of all the transactions to know if it is feasible.

You can now wait until the expiration in August or try to roll again after a few days for September. You didn't get rid of the option contract; you just added more credit, which is excellent, plus you increased the trade's commitment time.

That's rolling, but there are other possibilities, such as selling the August option OTM for less credit if you want to keep the shares. Or selling the August option more ITM to increase the credit received, which increases the chance of assignment/exercise because the probability of the option ending up ITM will be higher.

I'll explain more about this in the "rolling definition" section.

4.10   Rolling Down When the Underlying Share Price Falls

Imagine that, right after you have executed the trade, selling the covered call, the stock price suffers a very sharp drop. In this case, if you applied the rule of collecting 50% profit when the option loses value, you quickly collected $1.62, half of the $3.24.

If the stock continues to fall, a new (second) option further down can be sold again, with a strike price ATM near the current share price, in July, the same expiration month of the first call sold, which could be sold for about $3, unit value. Imagine that the investor can repeat this three times before the expiration date on July 16, 2021.

You close (buy back) the first option sold with 50% profit. Right after, sell another (second) option; if the stock keeps falling, the same happens again, and you buy this option back with 50% profit. You can then sell the third option in the following month, August. See the calculations below.

First sale - Option expires in July 2021
$3.24 per option sold x 100: $324
Profit of 50%: $162

Second sale - Option expires in July 2021
$3 per option sold x 100: $300
50% profit: $150

Third sale - Option expires in August 2021
Imagine that the stock had a sharp decline and was quoted at $415 when you sold this option.

This option is sold for $6 and expires in the following month, in August, a total amount of $600 referring to the 100 shares, strike price $415 ATM.

So instead of closing this third option contract with 50% profit, you let the contract go to the end because you will be assigned and will have to sell the shares for $415 each, but will keep the total premium amount of $600.

Now, let's do the math of all transactions, remembering that there are 100 shares equivalent to an option contract:

The initial cost of buying the shares: $42,361
The final selling value of the shares: $41,500
Loss on the shares: -$861
Total received in Premiums: $912 ($162 + $150 + $600)

The final profit is $51 (total premium $912 - $861 loss on the shares).

These are simulations and depend on the exact moment these operations are executed, but as the asset price plunges, options price more than doubles and may even triple because of the volatility. This is a way to manage risk and defend a position.

We saw that even with the stock devaluing by more than 2%, from $423.61 to $415, it is still possible to profit.

But, as I mentioned earlier, the ideal is to buy shares of good companies. Therefore, you do not need to apply this rolling technique. However, I decided to simulate this strategy here so that you, the reader, are aware of all the possibilities of managing risk that the options offer.

4.11　Rolling - Definition

Let's see the definition and the types of rolling techniques in the options market. As I mentioned in the previous section, rolling is when the investor closes one option position and immediately opens another one, using the same asset and option type.

4.11.1　Roll Forward or Out

When an option is rolled forward, closing the current position and opening a new one in the next month (ahead) or the next expiration cycle, where the premium is higher, this also increases your commitment time with the option contract.

This procedure is done to add more premium to the position. The longer the duration of the option contract, the higher its value.

For example, imagine that today is July 2, 2021, and that you have an open option that you sold a few weeks ago. This option expires on July 16, 2021, in two weeks.

❖ (1) Initial sale of the call for $1, unit value, a total of $100, sold a few weeks ago.

❖ (2) Today, July 2, 2021, the option may be worth $0.50 (in profit) or $1.50 (in loss). It will depend on whether the underlying share has valued or devalued. Either way, the position will be closed for a profit or a loss.

❖ (3) Next, you sell a new option with the same exercise price, of the same asset, in the month ahead, in August, for $2.50.

Being in August, a month ahead, this option is more expensive. If the first option sold is in profit, it will add more credit; the additional premium may cover the loss if you are losing money on the first option sold.

You also added more time—a month more—to your commitment to the option contract, which was due to expire in two weeks and has now been extended to approximately six weeks.

Parts one and two above are just a transaction of opening and closing an option trade position. Part three is like a new position started.

4.11.2   Roll Down

Rolling down means closing the current position and opening a new one in the same expiring month with a lower strike price.

Imagine that we are in November and that you sold an option that expires in approximately five weeks, in December. After a week, the option loses value, and you reach your goal.

❖ (1) Initial sale of the call for $1 - strike price $50.

❖ (2) The stock depreciates the following week, and the option loses value quickly, now worth $0.50. You then repurchase the option with a profit of 50% and completely exit the option contract.

❖ (3) You could do nothing, but as there are approximately four weeks left in the current cycle of options that expire in December, it is enough time that it still pays a reasonable premium. So you then decide to sell a new option for maybe $1 or $1.50 in the same month of December, but with a lower strike price, for example, $48.

Then, the option was rolled down from the exercise price from $50 to $48 in the same expiration cycle in December.

Parts one and two above are just a start and end option position. Part three is a new starting position.

4.11.3   Roll Up

Rolling up means closing the current position and opening a new one in the same expiring month with a higher exercise price. If, for example, you sold a call with a $50 strike price, which expires in December, to roll this option up, you need to repurchase it, exiting or closing the operation.

Then, a new position starts, which is to sell another call, which expires in the same cycle, in December, but with a higher strike price, for example, $52. Thus, the option was rolled up, from the exercise price of $50 to $52, in the same expiration cycle.

It might be difficult, in this case, to roll and add more credit. This strategy is used if the investor decides that they do not want to sell the stock. The investor should simply close the option trade on profit or loss, depending on whether the stock has valued or depreciated. But rolling up decreases the chance of assignment.

There is also the possibility of making a combination: for example, roll up to a higher exercise price and roll out in the next month or cycle, thus adding a higher credit.

Again, rolling is nothing more than completely exiting an option position and then starting a new one.

Important! If for some reason, you want to sell your shares (underlying asset of the option contract) and don't want to wait until the option expires, you have to close the option first and then sell the asset. Keeping the option open and selling the stock is another strategy (naked selling), which is much riskier.

4.11.4   Alternative

Instead of rolling immediately, the investor can close the initial position for a profit or loss and wait for the best time to sell another option contract.

For example, if the stock depreciates after starting the sale of the covered call, the investor can buy the option back cheaper to realize a profit, as we've seen in several examples in this book.

But instead of immediately selling a new option, as we saw in the section on rolling, the investor can wait for a better time when the stock increases in value and then sell calls again, OTM, thus enabling the sale of the new call with a higher strike price.

In addition to receiving an income from the sale of the option, the investor would also earn in the trading of the stock because the strike price, the value that the option seller is obliged to sell their shares, in case of appreciation, will be higher.

It is always worth remembering that the further away from the money, the lower the option's value, and that you want to sell expensive and buy back cheaper. See the chart in Figure 13 of the company Suzano, as an example.

Figure 13. SUZB3 - Source Trading View - 11/29/2019

Imagine if you bought the share at point 1 in Figure 13 for the value of $34 and sold a call OTM, for example, at the strike price of $35 and received the premium of $1, in unit values.

Notice that the stock depreciates over the following seven days. This option could have been repurchased for $0.50 or $50 for every 100 shares, a quick profit, instead of waiting until the expiration day.

With the stock losing value, you can keep selling calls, but it is better to sell calls with an exercise price of at least $34, which is the price you paid for the shares. But with the stock below $32, the exercise price of $34 is way OTM, and it may not have enough premium.

In this case, you can wait for the asset to rise again, as in point 2 of Figure 13, in which the stock valued and is back near $34, now you can start selling calls again.

The premium for the strikes prices of, for example, $34, $35, or $36, are much higher now, with a share at $34 compared to when it was at $32.

4.12   Why Close the Option with 50% Profit?

I had in portfolio shares of Suzano company and decided to sell some call option contracts, thus applying the covered call strategy. I did not use the rule of repurchasing the option with 50% profit and decided to wait until the option contract expired.

But if I had applied the rule, I would certainly have had a better result because I could have sold more options within the same expiration cycle. See Figure 14 below.

Figure 14. Example SUZB3 - Source - TradingView 11/21/2019

When I initiated the trade, I sold each call contract equivalent to 100 shares for $100 ($1 unit value) when the share price was at point 1 of the chart.

The share price was slightly above $34, and I sold the options at the strike price of $35, due in October 2019.

At point 2 of the chart, the share depreciated, and the call contract that I sold for $100 fell to less than $30. I could have repurchased it and made a profit of $70, but I decided to wait until expiration to profit the total value of $100.

After a few days, the stock rose again and came again close to $34. The same call contract that had lost value and gone down to $30 was now worth about $100 again, point 3 of the chart. If I had realized the profit of $70, mentioned above, I would have been free of the option contract at this point, and now, at point 3, I could have sold a new call for about $100.

This new call could have been repurchased for about $50 or $30 at point 4 of the chart, where the option was once again lost value because of the fall in the asset price.

At point five of the chart, I could have sold a new covered call, which would expire in November.

See that, from point 1 to 4 on the chart, approximately 17 days prior. If I had applied the rule to close the option with 50% profit, I could have done multiple transactions in the same expiration cycle in October 2019 instead of just one.

Point on chart	Trade	value
1	Sells (to open the position)	$100
2	Buy (to close the position)	$50
3	Sells (to open the position)	$100
4	Buy (to close the position)	$50

Table 9. "Why close the option with 50% profit"?

But I was determined to take the contract until the end (expiration) since the sale of the first option. Thus, at expiration, in October, the stock closed above $35, and I had to sell my shares at this price and kept only the total premium of $100.

Several studies show that, for the option seller, it is not worth waiting until expiration. Closing or repurchasing the option with 50% profit is the most efficient strategy in the long run.

The research team of Tastytrade, an American company specialized in options and with a team of data scientists, has done numerous studies, and all indicate that, for the seller, closing or exiting the option before expiration generates a higher return than waiting until the expiration date. This is because an option contract that is worth $100 can quickly devalue close to zero long before expiration.

The studies confirm what I already mentioned: I sold an option contract for $100 and could have repurchased it for $30. However, I did not do it, and the contract was again worth $100.

Another advantage pointed out in the studies is that closing before expiration decreases the time for which your capital or shares is allocated in the transaction; remember, your shares are covering you.

For example, you sell a call for $100, which expires in 45 days, and when you choose to repurchase it for $50 (50% profit), that position can be closed in 10 or 15 days if the stock doesn't appreciate much. Instead of waiting 45 days until expiration, you exit the trade well before and can wait for a new and reasonable opportunity to sell the calls again.

Remember the well-known phrase: time is money.

4.13   Close the Option with 70% Profit

Instead of closing the option with 50% profit, you can choose another percentage, such as 70%. In this case, simply multiply the premium initially received by 0.30. For instance, an initial premium of $100 multiplied by 0.30 is equal to $30. In this example, if the option was initially sold for $100, it has to be bought back for $30 to get a profit of 70%.

Obviously, the target value of 50% profit will be achieved faster than that of 70%. Therefore, by opting for 70% profit, the time your asset will be tied to the option will be longer. If you prefer not to close the option before expiration, you can wait until the option expires, as we saw earlier.

4.14   Sale of Covered Call - At-the-Money

Investors who do not mind selling some of their assets, as they may be at their target selling price, might prefer to sell the call covered with the at-the-money call (ATM), or even with the in-the-money (ITM), This is because, in this way, the probability of selling their shares is higher and they will get paid more to sell their assets, I mean a higher premium.

Let's go back to our Procter & Gamble example where we selected three options:

- ❖ Strike 130 - ITM (in-the-money)
- ❖ Strike 135 - ATM (at-the-money)
- ❖ Strike 140 - OTM (out-of-money)

PG	▼	PROCTER & GAMBLE CO COM	**134.79**	.05 -0.04%	B: 134.65 A: 134.90	ETB NYSE	⁺⁺ ±0.623	

⌄ Underlying						
>	Last X	Net Chng	Bid X	Ask X	Size	Volum
	134.79 N	-.05	134.65 P	134.90 P	3 x 2	6,200,78

> Trade Grid

⌄ Option Chain   Days to exp.: **32 - max**   Spread: **Single**   Layout: **Delta, Gamma, Theta, Vega**

		CALLS					Strikes: 10 ▼	
	Delta	Gamma	Theta	Vega	Bid X	Ask X	Exp	Strike
⌄ 16 JUL 21	(37) 100							
	.94	.00	-.02	.05	24.40 N	25.55 P	16 JUL 21	110
	.93	.01	-.02	.05	19.25 P	20.75 N	16 JUL 21	115
	.92	.01	-.02	.06	14.70 X	15.40 Z	16 JUL 21	120
	.86	.03	-.02	.10	10.05 X	10.60 X	16 JUL 21	125
	.73	.04	-.03	.14	5.65 Q	6.10 X	16 JUL 21	130
	.48	.06	-.03	.17	2.52 B	2.60 B	16 JUL 21	135
	.21	.04	-.02	.13	.76 Z	.79 B	16 JUL 21	140
	.07	.02	-.01	.06	.21 Z	.24 X	16 JUL 21	145
	.03	.01	-.01	.03	.08 Z	.10 Z	16 JUL 21	150
	.02	.00	.00	.02	.04 Z	.06 Z	16 JUL 21	155

Figure 15. Procter & Gamble - Source: Thinkorswim Platform

But now we will choose the ATM option, which is the strike $135.

❖ Strike: $135

❖ Delta 0.48

❖ Premium $2.52 (one contract): Total $252. Imagine we lowered the price from $2.60 to $2.52 to get this order filled.

❖ Expires in 37 days.

The premium is higher, and delta 0.48 is also higher than the delta of the strike $140. The delta of 0.48 also means there is approximately a 48% chance that the stock will close above this value in the 37 days.

The ATM options are the ones with the most extrinsic value, the ATM strike $135 has an intrinsic of $0.21, and the extrinsic value is $2.31.

Compared to the $130 strike (ITM) with $4.79 intrinsic and the remainder extrinsic value of only $0.86, the total option price is $5.65 calculated by the intrinsic plus the extrinsic value, already explained in this book.

With more practice and experience, the investor will be able to determine and better choose the exercise price to be sold ITM, ATM, or OTM.

4.15 Sale of the Covered Call - In-the-Money - Leverage

Implementing the strategy with the sale of the call ITM, as we saw earlier, provides greater protection, but the earning potential is lower.

However, this strategy can become more attractive with the use of margin or leverage. Some brokers offer the purchase of the share on a fixed-term or margin, where the investor initially disburses 50% or 30% of the total purchase value, such as a loan.

Imagine if your broker finances 70% of the value for you to buy shares, such as P&G, in Figure 15 before. As shown in the figure, the share price is $134.79, and the total of 100 shares is $13,479.

In this scenario, you would disburse only 30% of this amount, $4,043.70, and if you sell the ITM call with a strike price of $130, you will have the following result:

- ❖ Amount invested: $4,043.70
- ❖ Strike: $130
- ❖ Premium $5.65 (one contract): Total $565
- ❖ Expires (time) in 37 days.

If, at the end of the 37 days, the share is quoted above the value of the strike price of $130, this will be the final result of the operation.

Purchase and sale of shares: Loss of $479 ($13,000 - $13,479)
Premium received: $565
Profit: $86 ($565 - $479).

The return on this strategy is 2.13% in just 37 days—a figure calculated by the profit of $86 divided by the initial investment of $4,043.70.

The normal transaction without the margin would make the profit of $86 divided by the full total amount of the 100 shares $13,479, which gives a return of 0.64% in 37 days.

The brokerage costs and charges for this transaction have not been included.

4.16   Placing the trade on the Online-Broker

Now, let's see how to perform the transaction using the ThinkorSwim Platform. For this example, let's choose Apple, code AAPL.

Selling the call on a stock you already own

If you already own Apple shares, you can sell the call on your shares; it will be covered because you already own the stock. Notice the highlighted area in Figure 10.

The last stock price was $127.35 and, on the field spread, I selected "Single" for a single sale of the call because, in this example, I already hold the stock; the chosen strike is $135 for the premium of $2.35.

Once you have checked all the details, you can press the confirm and send button at the bottom.

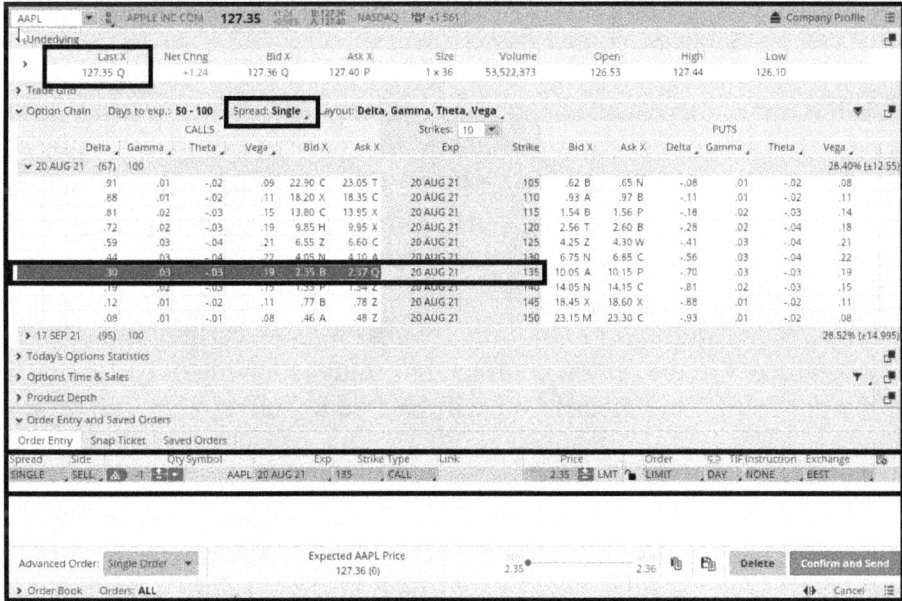

Figure 10. Selling the call only (covered)

This operation is selling to open; the order is "limit" to be filled at the minimum price of $2.35 or better. The option "day" is selected. This means the order will be active on the broker platform until it reaches the price of $2.35 for all day. If instead of "day", you can change it to "GTC", which means good until cancel, the order will be open for many days until it reaches the price desired of a minimum of $2.35.

Once the order is executed, to close the position, like the example of the 50% profit target, you have to buy it to close to finish (exit) this position or wait until the expiration date.

Let's say you want to do the 50% profit target. After the order is filled, you select it and choose to buy to close for the price of $1.17 limit order and "GTC" good until close.

This means that the order will be open in the broker's system until the option loses value and reaches the desired purchase price of $1.17. As the value of the options varies widely, with a fall in the share price, this price can be reached in a few days or weeks.

If the option depreciates and reaches the price of $1.17, the order is executed. After the execution, you will no longer have any open options position because you initially sold the call for $2.35 to open or enter the trade and then repurchased the same option for $1.17, half the price, to get out and close this trade.

Thus, the profit is $117 ($1.17 x 100), as we saw earlier, and you are now totally out of the option contract, returning to having only the shares in the portfolio. This means you will be free to sell another call at any time.

Always review the order before executing it. Ensure you are in the right tab to start the "sell" position and exit "buy". Mistakes happen, and you don't want to sell a second call without having the shares in the portfolio (naked option), which is a much riskier strategy.

The above procedure varies from broker to broker. First, check how to execute the option trade order with your broker.

Simultaneously buying the stock and selling the call

This time I selected the same option, but on the spread field, the strategy chosen was covered stock, as shown in Figure 11 below. Thus, in this transaction, I will buy the stock and sell the call option at the same time.

Notice that the bid and ask spread now is for the purchase of the stock and the sale of the call together. On the confirm tab below, the debit for this transaction will be $125, which includes the purchase of the stock for $127.35 minus the premium received for the call $2.35. Thus, the total net debit is $125 in unit values.

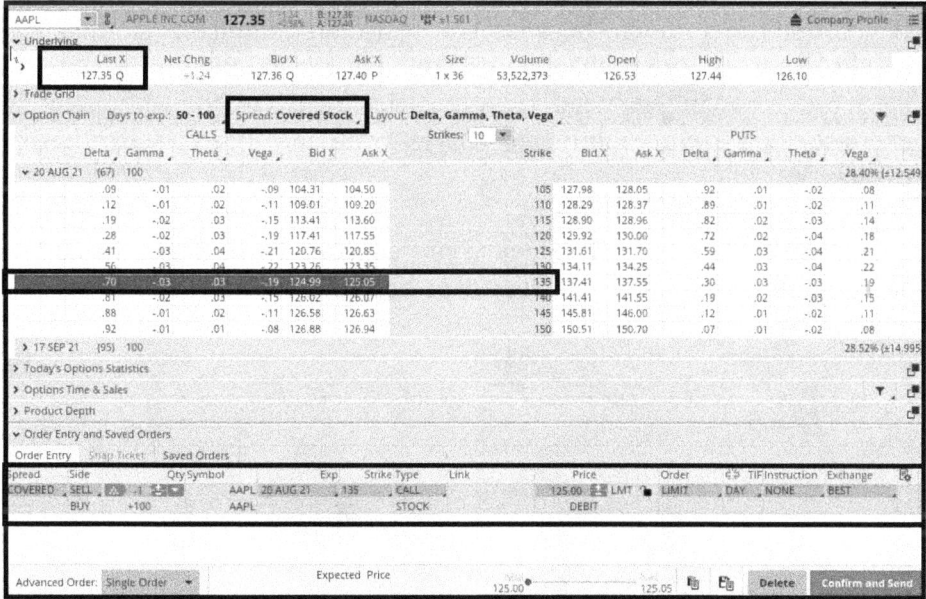

Figure 11. Buying the stock and selling the call

Brokerage costs

When implementing this strategy, it is imperative to be aware of the costs to open and close the trades and assignment costs. These costs can affect profits dramatically.

4.17 Early Assignment and Dividend Risk

Risk of an assignment before expiration. If you, the investor, who sold the option, do not want to sell the stock, this explanation is fundamental. If you don't care much, because you chose an exercise price that you would like to sell your shares, you don't have to be too concerned, but it's worth knowing in what situations the owner of the option might exercise their right to buy the shares from the option seller before expiration.

See the example of PBR stock (Petroleo Brasileiro), Figure 16 below. Note that it is only three calendar days before the June 18, 2021 options expire.

PBR		PETROLEO BRASILEIRO SA ADR SPONSORED	**11.52**	0.00%	B: 11.21 A: 11.79	NYSE	

∨ Underlying

	Last X	Net Chng	Bid X	Ask X	Size	Volume
>	11.52 N	0	11.21 K	11.79 P	1 x 5	N/A

> Trade Grid

∨ Option Chain   Filter: **Off**   Spread: **Single**   Layout: **Intrinsic, Extrinsic, Last X**

		CALLS				Strikes: 10	
	Intrinsic	Extrinsic	Last X	Bid X	Ask X	Exp	Strike
∨ 18 JUN 21 (3) 100							
	2.02	.01	1.99 N	1.96 B	2.10 T	18 JUN 21	9.5
	1.52	0	1.50 H	1.47 B	1.57 X	18 JUN 21	10
	1.02	.025	1.00 C	1.02 Q	1.07 B	18 JUN 21	10.5
	.52	.04	.55 N	.53 B	.59 B	18 JUN 21	11
	.02	.185	.21 P	.19 H	.22 B	18 JUN 21	11.5
	0	.065	.07 A	.06 H	.07 H	18 JUN 21	12
	0	.03	.02 Z	.02 H	.04 H	18 JUN 21	12.5
	0	.015	.01 B	0 D	.03 H	18 JUN 21	13
	0	.015	.02 Q	0 D	.03 H	18 JUN 21	13.5
	0	.005	.01 H	0 D	.01 H	18 JUN 21	14

Figure 16. PBR options chain. Source: thinkorswim platform

Look at the selected option with the strike price of $10. The extrinsic value or time value is zero because the option is deep ITM and with little time remaining.

The "last" column shows the last price at which the option was traded, $1.50. Let's calculate the intrinsic value, which is the share value of $11.52, minus the strike price of $10. Thus, what we have is an intrinsic value of $1.52.

Therefore, the total cost of the option is composed only of intrinsic value because the option is trading equal to or a little below the intrinsic value.

This option has no extrinsic value (time value). Most of the time, options are exercised at expiration, but this option can be exercised at any time, even before expiration.

In the ITM section, I explained that call option holders do not exercise when the options have time or time value. In this case, it is different; the option no longer has a time value.

Dividend risk is the risk of assignment for the call seller, even when the option still has extrinsic value or time value. The risk is when the company announces a dividend if the value of this dividend is greater than the option's extrinsic value.

Still, in Figure 16, see the strike $11. The total value of the option in the "last" column is $0.55. This value comprises the intrinsic value of $0.52 (share price, $11.52, minus the strike price, $11) and the extrinsic value, which is the remainder, $0.03 or nearly $0.04.

If it is the ex-dividend date and the company announces a dividend of $0.10 per share, an amount that is much higher than the extrinsic value of $0.04 of the option, the holder of this option will most likely exercise the right to buy before expiration, because the value of the dividend is greater than the extrinsic value (time value) of the option.

When the option stays ITM and with little time remaining until expiration, a week, for example, the risk of early assignment is high. If the company announces a dividend and it is greater than the option's extrinsic value, the chance of exercise is much higher.

The risk of exercise is only for American-style options because they can be exercised at any time by the call buyer. This risk does not exist for European-style options, as they can only be exercised on the last day when the option contract expires.

If the option is deep ITM and if the investor does not want to sell the shares, they can roll over to the following month with more time or time value: the extrinsic value of the following month will be higher and decrease the risk of exercise.

It is worth remembering that, if there is exercise, this means that the strategy worked because, in fact, the sale of the covered call is a bullish strategy. You sold the stock at a higher strike or exercise price at a profit and still received a premium. Would you rather see your stocks depreciate? So, exercise is not a thing to lose sleep over.

If the options expire ITM, the shares will disappear from your account on the day after expiration. Check the costs your broker charges in case of assignment.

If the option has expired ITM, but the stock remains in your account, check with the broker, as the process may take two or three days. Do not think that the option has not been exercised and that you can already sell a new call, as you may be selling a naked option, which is much riskier.

4.18 Tips

In the beginning, while you are learning, it is a good idea to create a spreadsheet to record the profit of your options sold and analyze the performance of this strategy.

Start by selling only one contract to practice. Then, with more experience, increase the number of contracts sold. But remember, for every 100 shares in the portfolio, you can sell an option contract.

Monitor the sold option the same way you observe the stock price; in doing so, you will better understand how the options price is affected.

4.19 Summary of Implementing the Strategy

❖ The strategy can be initiated with the shares that the investor already holds in their portfolio or with a simultaneous operation, in which first, the stock is bought and then the call option is sold.

❖ Selling the call without holding the shares is a high-risk strategy, classified as naked selling.

❖ The option to be sold can be in-the-money (ITM), at-the-money (ATM) or out-of-the-money (OTM). The delta can be used as a reference to choose the option to be sold.

❖ The ideal is to sell options with 45 calendar days to expiration. However, it can be between 60 and 30 days.

❖ Sell the option for a credit to open the position, then repurchase the option for a debit, with 50% or 70% profit, to close the position, or wait until expiration.

❖ The return on investment is calculated by the amount of the final premium received, divided by the cost or average cost of the shares, then multiplied by 100 to convert to the percentage.

❖ Use rolling techniques to add more premium and time.

❖ American-style options, with no extrinsic value, can be exercised before expiration. If there is an announcement of dividends, the risk is higher.

5

Reasons to Use this Strategy

You've probably heard people say that options are very risky instruments; most of the time, what happens is that people want easy and fast money—they want to buy an option as if it were a lottery ticket and end up losing money. And they also don't invest in learning and, as a result, give up one of the most powerful investment strategies.

With the examples and explanations that have been presented so far, I can highlight the following advantages that the sale of the covered call offers:

5.1 Cost and Risk Reduction

As I showed in the examples, each time you sell a covered call, the premium is instantly deposited into your brokerage account. If you bought 100 shares for $3,000 and sold a call contract for $200, you automatically had your share costs reduced to $2,800. This way, you are already in front of other investors who only bought the stock.

The cost reduction coincides with the risk reduction because now, using the example above, the risk you have on the table is $2,800, reduced by $200.

There is a lot of talk about buying a put option as a way to secure the stock. There are several problems with this strategy:

❖ The cost of a put option can erode the gains you have earned on dividends or with asset appreciation.

❖ It is extremely difficult to predict when the market will decline, the market timing. Imagine if you buy a put (insurance) for 30 days, and a week after the put expired, a fall in the market occurs, and you are unprotected. In addition to these losses, you also have to add all the costs associated with purchasing the insurance (the put).

❖ Again, the sale of the covered call helps to reduce the initial cost of the asset, which consequently reduces the risk. Thus, we take advantage of insurance paid by another person, the buyer of the call.

5.2 Time Value and Compound Interest

Time value is defined as a dollar received today worth more than a dollar received tomorrow. Would you rather receive some return from your shares, such as dividends, today or ten months from now?

Use the compound interest, reinvest and multiply earnings by selling the covered call. The money received for the sale of the call will be available in your account on the next day, depending on the broker. Then it can be used immediately to buy more shares or be applied to any other investment, such as fixed income.

The sooner the money starts working for you, the better. The intention is for these small, consistent profits to transform and grow your portfolio.

5.3 Study - OCC (Options Clearing Corporation)

A study by the Options Clearing Corporation (OCC) in the United States found some important facts about the sale of the covered call.

The study, entitled "15 years of study of the Russell 2000 index," compared the purchase of only the shares of the index, with the strategy of selling the covered call, which is the purchase of the shares of the index and the sale of the call.

Using 2% out-of-the-money (OTM) options with a month to expire, the covered call selling strategy outperformed the Russell index alone and with lower volatility in yields. However, the advantage did not last when options that expired in two months were used.

Another study, "The performance of options-based investment strategies," analyzed, during the period 2003-2013, the ten most liquid shares on the U.S. stock exchange and tested several options strategies. It was found that the sale of the covered call often outperforms the performance of other options strategies.

Meanwhile, Hewitt EnnisKnupp revised the Index, symbol BXM, a benchmark index consisting of buying the shares of the S&P 500 index and selling the call option, i.e., the covered call strategy.

Hewitt EnnisKnupp found that from 1986 to 2012, the BXM index had returns aligned with the S&P itself and with a decrease in volatility. But, in sharply high markets, BXM generally underperformed the S&P, which does not use the sale of the covered call.

However, the BMX fund automatically sells the call every third Friday of each month and keeps the option until it expires. That's part of the fund's rules. You, the investor, don't have to follow these rules.

As I mentioned earlier, you can expect a rise in stocks and then sell the call for a higher exercise price. Plus, you can enjoy all of the flexibilities I explain in this book, such as closing the option before expiration, rolling, and many more.

6

Other Important Factors

6.1 Warning

This is a low-risk but not risk-free strategy. The risk exists, and that is in the fall in the asset price.

Please don't buy a stock for the simple fact that it has options available. Stick to your buying criteria. The ideal is always to apply this strategy to companies that have the best financial indicators, which are good deals to invest in. Do your homework: do your own analysis about the stock or use the analysis services of a research firm.

This strategy is no guarantee of success, but we are definitely putting the odds of frequent profits in our favor.

6.2 Economic Environment

In case of a favorable economic environment and expectation of economic growth, it would be wise to wait for the stock to value and then start applying the covered call out of money to generate a better income.

In the case of pessimism, it would be better to sell the call closer to the money. That's just an opinion, of course!

6.3 Binary Events: News and Earnings Results

News, important events and earning results are known as binary events, as assets can value or depreciate quickly.

See Figure 17, which shows that, in October 2019, the firm Localiza reported an excellent net profit of $204 million. Even then, the stock devalued after the disclosure because the market expected a better number in addition to other factors.

Figure 17. RENT3 Action Locates - Source: TradingView

Suzano (SUZB3), a Brazilian stock, reported a loss of $3.46 billion in the third quarter of 2019.

Figure 18. SUZB3 Suzano. Source: TradingView

Note that, in Figure 18, point 1 is a date close to the announcement of the results. Even with the reported loss, the stock had a strong appreciation in the following days.

Events, such as the earning results, are considered binary and should be avoided if the investor intends to start the strategy simultaneously, which is the purchase of the share and sale of the call.

The investor who owns stocks in the portfolio can take advantage of these events because many traders buy options to speculate. With increased demand, volatility also increases, and the price of options can triple.

On the day of the event, the prices of the options are high. A premium worth $2 may be worth $6 or more at the same strike price. Often, if nothing exceptional happens after the result, maybe on the same day or the next day, the option that was priced at $6 might now be worth $2.

If the investor applies the rule of closing the operation with 50% profit, the investor can get a good return in a very short time frame.

This is the phenomenon of volatility, which is known as "mean reversion". It indicates that a stock has some high volatility peaks, but that historically, the volatility of the stock always returns to its historical or normal average. This can also be considered as trading volatility.

6.4 Tax

In addition to the brokerage costs, you must check how options are taxed in your country. You might have to pay tax on the premium you received when selling an option. If you buy options to speculate, you will probably have to pay capital gain tax.

6.5 Liquidity

We've all heard of someone who needed to sell something quickly like a cell phone, house, car, or even a company—or we might even have faced this ourselves. To find a buyer and convert these things into money as soon as possible, in this scenario, most probably, the item had to be sold for a lower price than it was worth.

This is the problem with the lack of liquidity: when we want to sell something, and we have a product that few people are interested in buying, the price has to be reduced so that we can do business.

In the financial market, as well as in any market, the same concept applies. Therefore, we have to try to choose assets with liquid options.

The options with the highest traded volumes are the most liquid. In the options chain, you can see the traded volume.

Figure 19 shows the option chains for Apple, stock code AAPL. It displays the volume and the open interest.

The higher the volume and open interest, the higher the liquidity. Note the highlighted strike of $135; this option has the higher volume and open interest of all options for APPL that expires on July 16, 2021.

AAPL	▾	🗓 APPLE INC COM	**129.6701**	-.8099 -0.62%	▲ 129.68	ETB	NASDAQ	⚌ ±0.528	

✔ Underlying						
›	Last X	Net Chng	Bid X	Ask X	Size	Volume
	129.6701 D	-.8099	129.67 Q	129.68 Z	7 x 11	5,012,784

› Trade Grid

✔ Option Chain   Days to exp.: **30 - 100**   Spread: **Single**   Layout: **Volume, Open Interest**

		CALLS			Strikes: 10 ▾		
	Volume	Open.Int	Bid X	Ask X		Exp	Strike
✔ 16 JUL 21	(31) 100						
	19	1,735	24.75 Z	24.90 B		16 JUL 21	105
	3	23,524	19.85 B	20.00 I		16 JUL 21	110
	19	16,541	15.00 P	15.15 C		16 JUL 21	115
	6	46,263	10.30 C	10.45 Z		16 JUL 21	120
	726	71,554	6.20 W	6.25 Z		16 JUL 21	125
	1,284	112,729	3.00 Z	3.05 Z		16 JUL 21	130
	2,183	166,940	1.20 N	1.21 Z		16 JUL 21	135
	1,469	103,908	.44 Z	.45 Q		16 JUL 21	140
	469	51,873	.20 Z	.21 Z		16 JUL 21	145
	224	38,493	.12 Z	.13 Z		16 JUL 21	150

Figure 19. Liquidity AAPL stock. Source: thinkorswim platform

There is another way to know if the option is liquid or not. Check the difference between the bid and ask prices, the bid/ask spread. This rule applies to any financial instrument.

Let's check Figure 19 again and compare a high liquid option with a less liquid one.

We already know that the strike of $135 is the most liquid; if we look at the difference between the bid/ask spread, it is only one cent, the best offer to sell is 1.21, and the best offer to buy is 1.20 cents. This is characteristic of extremely liquid assets.

However, the difference in the bid/ask spread with the in-the-money (ITM) option strike of $105 is fifteen cents, which shows that this is a less liquid option. Spreads where the difference between the bid and ask price is larger than ten cents are more concerning and should be avoided.

Some stocks have more liquid options than others; your job is to find high liquidity stock to trade options and find liquid options on those stocks.

Blank Page

7

The Australian Options Market

The Australia Stock Exchange (ASX) first started offering options for Australian stocks in 1976. Although still a small market, there are some stocks that you can sell covered calls.

Most traded stock options on ASX (May 2021)
At the time of writing, the following are the most traded stock on the Australia Exchange. Note that, on the top of the list is the index of the ASX 200, code XJO.

Options - Top Classes by Volume

RANK	MAY 21	VOLUME[1]	% MKT	OPEN INTEREST	VOL/OP
1	XJO	408,645	10.1%	222,985	183.3%
	CBA	339,573	8.4%	89,943	377.5%
3	BHP	324,308	8.0%	168,787	192.1%
4	FMG	296,253	7.3%	94,113	314.8%
5	WBC	237,194	5.9%	154,072	154.0%
6	TLS	231,622	5.7%	256,525	90.3%
7	ANZ	226,185	5.6%	148,186	152.6%
8	NCM	199,323	4.9%	76,158	261.7%
9	NAB	189,694	4.7%	144,860	130.9%
10	RIO	177,765	4.4%	51,855	342.8%
11	AWC	137,677	3.4%	97,623	141.0%
12	WPL	109,871	2.7%	82,652	132.9%
13	S32	108,175	2.7%	64,966	166.5%
14	IPL	89,932	2.2%	44,697	201.2%
15	STO	84,741	2.1%	52,101	162.6%

Figure 20. Most Traded Options in Australia May 21. Source: ww2.asx.com.au

7.1 Liquidity Risk

One of the advantages of the covered call strategy is that the option might lose liquidity after initiating the trade or getting close to the expiration date.

If that happens, you let the trade run until the end, and if the option expires OTM, you keep the premium. If the option expires ITM, you sell your shares and keep the premium, as already explained in sections 4.4 and 4.6.

For those who trade other types of structured options strategies, like spreads, this might be a major issue because you are dealing with a multiple options leg strategy in addition to the liquidity problem.

Note that not every stock has options available. Actually, on the ASX, there are only a few stocks that have options available to trade. It is up to the exchange to decide which company options to list on and make available to the public. A full list of tradable stock options in Australia and quotes are available on asx.com.au/options.

7.2 Broker Costs

One of the main issues in Australia, as in many countries outside the USA, might be the costs to trade; with all the traditional banks that offer a trading platform, the prices are very high, around AU$35 to start a position and another AU$35 to close it.

You have to go to the ASX website to find a list of the brokerage companies authorized to offer options in Australia and look for a good deal.

You will find some alternatives, like the Interactive Brokers that charge only about $2 to open and another $2 to close it, but you might have to pay a small monthly fee. You have to do some research to find the best alternative.

I have a referral link from Interactive Brokers; you might get some bonus with this link: https://ibkr.com/referral/rubens484

Blank Page

8

Farewell

I'd like to thank you for taking the time to read my first book. I decided to embark on this project because I wanted to work on something that I like: the options market.

I've been operating options since 2015, and I know that selling the covered call is one of the strategies that works. To confirm my opinion and experience, I researched the best materials available in the world on this topic—books and websites—and included all that valuable information in this book.

In addition to confirming effectiveness, I have also delivered a complete explanation of how to implement and manage this strategy in this book. Therefore, I am sure that you now have an excellent tool to help you obtain better returns on your investments.

I have mentioned various scenarios for implementing the strategy and multiple ways to manage it, such as closing before expiration, rolling, leverage, etc. So, you can see the flexibility that options strategies offer and how you can use your creativity to manage your investments.

I hope I have helped you better understand this fascinating world of options. Be patient when it comes to learning. I recommend that you read the entire book and, after a few days or weeks, go back and read the parts that you did not fully understand.

Also, look for more information on the internet, it will help a lot. I'll also leave my contact details below so you can get in touch.

Last but not least, I would like to thank my friends from Sydney in Australia; Julio Weber and his Yunqin Wang and also Rosie Rogge for their comments and suggestions that helped me to improve this book.

See you soon,
Rubens De Souza

Instagram: rubens_sza
Instagram: thestrategistinvest
Twitter: rubens_sza
THESTRATEGISTINVEST.COM

9

Extra Definitions

As I mentioned earlier, I've left the definition section to the end of the book to avoid complicating the explanation of the covered call. Below, I'll show you some definitions that will help you learn more about the options market—not only the covered call but also options in general.

9.1 Holder

The holder is the buyer of the option, which holds the right but not the obligation to buy the underlying asset, according to the terms of the contract.

9.2 Writer or Seller

The writer is the seller of the option, which receives the premium and has an obligation to comply with the contract terms.

9.3 Gamma and Rho

Gamma and rho are part of the Greeks, the different dimensions of risk involved in taking an options position. The rho refers to the change in the price of an option in relation to the interest rate. The influence of rho on the price of options is minimal, so very little is said about it.

Yet Gamma is an important Greek, because it measures the rate of change of the delta. It reflects how much the delta will increase or decrease in response to each movement of a point in the underlying asset price.

Imagine a stock that costs $40 and a call option with a $43 strike, which expires in 30 days. Suppose this option has a delta of 0.30 and a gamma of 0.10.

If the share price rises a dollar, from $40 to $41, the delta will be adjusted up by 0.10, increasing from 0.30 to 0.40. If the asset depreciates a dollar, the delta decreased by 0.10, from 0.30 to 0.20, because of the gamma of 0.10.

Gamma is the enemy of the option seller and friend of the buyer because it makes those options about to turn dust suddenly worth a lot. This happens with options that are close to expiring and that are at or near the money.

This phenomenon is known as "Gamma explosion", or "Gamma risk", for the options seller. For deep ITM options or far OTM, the effect of the range is minimal.

This risk is under control for us covered call sellers because we are covered, as the strategy's name says. The naked options seller, on the other hand, has to manage this risk well.

9.4 Delta Neutral

This is a portfolio management strategy or approach that uses multiple options positions to maintain a balance of positive and negative deltas so that the overall delta of the assets of the portfolio in question totals zero and thus decreases directional risk.

9.5 Put Option

The put option gives the owner the right to sell an asset (the underlying one) at a specified price, on a predetermined date (expiration), to a particular person (the seller of the put option).

The put is most used as stock insurance, or for speculation, for those who bet on the price fall of the asset.

9.6 Hedging

A hedge is a strategy to protect your finances from a risky situation, using options as insurance, diversification, or the future market. It is designed to minimize or compensate for the chance of your assets losing value.

9.7 Collar

To set up the collar, the investor implements the covered call strategy explained in this book (buy shares and sell the call) and then adds the purchase of a put; this is the collar. The put works as a hedge, making the strategy very safe and with very limited loss, but with a very low earning potential.

9.8 Synthetic

There are many synthetic options. They are used to recreate the profit and risk profile of a specific option or stock, using combinations of underlying assets or different options.

For example, one single share is equivalent to one delta: if the investor buys 100 shares of Apple, they will have 100 positive deltas in the portfolio.

To create a synthetic position, one can sell a put contract at-the-money (ATM) and buy a call contract ATM. Options ATM have a delta of 0.50; an option contract is equivalent to 100 shares.

So, the sale of a put-in-money option contract has 50 positive deltas and the purchase of a call ATM also has 50 positive deltas. In total, the two options have 100 positive deltas, thus equaling 100 deltas of the 100 shares. Therefore, both stocks, or the synthetic option, have the same risk and profit profile.

9.9 Options Spreads

A spread position is formed with the purchase and also the sale of another option of the same asset, but with different strike prices.

9.10 index

A market index is a hypothetical portfolio of investment holdings representing a segment of the financial market. The calculation of the index value comes from the prices of the assets that make up the index.

The most popular are the Indexes of the United States Dow Jones, SP&500, Nasdaq; in Brazil, the Ibovespa; and in Australia, the ASX 200.

9.11 ETF

It is an exchange-traded fund that usually tracks an underlying index, although it can invest in various industry sectors or use different strategies. ETFs are listed on exchanges, like shares traded throughout the day.

Blank Page

10

About the author:

Rubens Gonçalves De Souza holds a Business Administration and Foreign Trade degree from Mackenzie University in São Paulo in Brazil.

He also earned a degree in financial planning from Mentor Education in Australia and a certificate in Finance from Griffith University, also in Australia.

Rubens has been operating in the U.S. options market since 2015 and currently operates options in Australia, Brazil, and the United States.

11

References:

Ellman, Allan (2011) Complete Encyclopedia for Covered Call Writing. The blue collar investor, USA: Digital Publishing of Florida, Inc.

McMillan, G. Lawrence (2012) Options as a strategic investment, 5 edn. USA: Penguin Group (USA) Inc.

Sincere, Michael (2014) Understanding Options, 2 edn., USA: McGraw-Hill Education books.

Online:

Evan, My Journey to millions (2016). What is Time Decay and Why Do I Love It? What is time corrosion and why do I love it? Available in: https://www.myjourneytomillions.com/articles/time-decay-love/ (Accessed: 23/10/2019).

Wikipedia, the free encyclopedia (2009) Options market, available at: https://pt.wikipedia.org/wiki/Mercado_de_opções (Accessed: 23/10/2019).

Chen, James (2019) What Is an Option? Available in: https://https://www.investopedia.com/terms/o/option.asp (Accessed: 23/10/2019).

The Options Guide (2017) Gamma, dispoable in: https://www.theoptionsguide.com/gamma.aspx (Accessed: 28/10/2019).

Tastytrade (2018), Why Not Hold To Expiration ? Why not wait until Expiration? dispoable in: https://www.tastytrade.com/tt/shows/options-jive/episodes/why-not-hold-to-expiration-01-17-2018 (Accessed: 04/11/2019).

Tastytrade Covered Call, dispoable in: https://www.tastytrade.com/tt/learn/covered-call (Accessed: 07/11/2019).

Burns, Brian (2009) A Brief History of Stock Options, dispoable in: https://www.thestreet.com/opinion/a-brief-history-of-stock-options-10595277 (Accessed: 10/11/2019).

OptionsTrading.org (2017) The History of Options Trading, dispoable in: https://www.optionstrading.org/history/ (Accessed: 10/11/2019).

Cboe Global Markets, Inc. () Cboe S&P 500 BuyWrite Index (BXM), available at: http://www.cboe.com/products/strategy-benchmark-indexes/buywrite-indexes/cboe-s-p-500-buywrite-index-bxm (Accessed: 20/12/2019).

References:

The Options Industry Council (2018) Get the Facts about Covered Calls, available at: https://www.theocc.com/about/newsroom/blog/2018/Get-the-Facts-About-Covered-Calls.jsp (Accessed: 20/12/2019).

ASX (2021) Equity Derivatives Statistics, Available at: https://www2.asx.com.au/markets/trade-our-derivatives-market/overview/equity-derivatives/equity-derivatives-statistics (Accessed: 18/06/2021).

Tastytrade (2016) Why 45 DTE is the Magic Number - Because 45 days before it expires is the magic number, dispoable in: https://www.tastytrade.com/tt/shows/the-skinny-on-options-modeling/episodes/why-45-dte-is-the-magic-number-05-26-2016--2 (Access: 13/01/2019)

12

Index

W

Index